A John Catt Publication

Primary Computing in ACTION

Yasemin Allsop & Ben Sedman

First published 2015
by John Catt Educational Ltd,
12 Deben Mill Business Centre, Old Maltings Approach,
Melton, Woodbridge IP12 1BL
Tel: +44 (0) 1394 389850
Fax: +44 (0) 1394 386893
Email: enquiries@johncatt.com
Website: www.johncatt.com

Opinions expressed in this publication are those of the contributors
and are not necessarily those of the publishers or the editors.
We cannot accept responsibility for any errors or omissions.

ISBN: 978 1 909717 50 3

Set and designed by Theoria Design Ltd
www.theoriadesign.com

Printed and bound in Great Britain

Scratch is developed by the Lifelong Kindergarten Group at the MIT Media Lab.
See http://scratch.mit.edu

Contents

Foreword

The introduction of computing into the National Curriculum for England in 2014 presents opportunities and challenges. For primary schools rethinking how best to incorporate computing into the curriculum this book offers a wealth of tried and tested practical ways to develop children's computing skills. Whatever stage you might be in your career – from the beginning teacher to subject leader – this book has much to offer you as you consider how best to meet the needs of learners and statutory requirements in computing.

Drawing on the experience of educators with particular expertise and interest in computing and the use of ICT in education, the book includes advice on planning, teaching and assessment of the 2014 Computing Curriculum. Examples in the book show how to make creative use of freely available web based applications, programmes for PCs and Macs, and Apps to design an innovative and engaging curriculum across the full primary age range.

Each chapter includes structured suggestions for lessons, illustrating how computing can be embedded across the curriculum. The authors introduce an easy to implement rigorous and manageable approach to assessment that enables teachers to monitor and record learners' progress in computing.

This book is an essential resource for anyone who wants to make the most of the opportunities afforded by the entry of computing into the National Curriculum and is looking for support to meet the challenges this represents.

Sue Pope
Associate Head of Department
Primary Teacher Education
Manchester Metropolitan University

Author biographies

EDITORS

Yasemin Allsop worked as an ICT Coordinator in primary schools in London for almost 10 years. She is currently employed as a Senior Lecturer in Primary Computing and ICT at Roehampton University. She has an MA ICT in Education from the London Knowledge Lab, University of London. She is also an MPhil/PhD student, focusing on children's thinking, learning and metacognition when designing digital games. She has articles published widely in quality journals and has presented at conferences. She is the editor of an online magazine called ICT in Practice where educators from around the world share their experiences of using technology in education. Website: www.yaseminallsop.me.uk

Ben Sedman is a Senior Lecturer within the Faculty of Education at Manchester Metropolitan University. Previous to this role he taught for seven years within the primary sector. Ben currently teaches within the STEM Division at MMU, delivering primary D&T and computing sessions to trainees and teachers. He has completed his MA in Education, has been involved in a European funded project and helps coordinate the Erasmus Exchange Programme. Ben is interested in a range of creative teaching approaches and enjoys photography. Some of his work can be viewed at www.bensedmanphotography.com. This is his first book.

CONTRIBUTING AUTHORS

Alessandro Bogliolo is the coordinator of the School of Information Science and Technology of the University of Urbino, in Italy (www.informatica.uniurb.it). He teaches Computer Architecture and he coordinates research activities in the fields of wireless sensor networks, mobile applications, and green cloud computing. In 2013 he founded Code's Cool (www.codescool.net), an open online learning community where pupils and parents can meet university students and teachers to code together. Since 2013 he has served as Europe Code Week Ambassador in Italy (www.codeweek.it). In 2014 he coordinated a pan European crowdcoding experiment leading to the development of an Android game called FlagShip (www.flagshipgame.eu). In November 2014 he launched CodyRoby (www.codeweek.it/cody-roby-en). Since 2015 he coordinates the group of Code Week Ambassadors organizing Europe Code Week (www.codeweek.eu).

Ahmet Çelik is currently working in The Distance Education Applied & Research Center of Gazi University, in Turkey. He has got B.Ed. and M.Ed. degrees from Computer Education & Instructional Technology department and he is currently a Ph.D. candidate in the same department. Ahmet also has articles and books published in Turkish, one of the books is called *Three Dimensional (3D) Design for Kids*. His research interests are distance education, instructional design, technology education for kids and early entrepreneurship education for kids. In recent years he has been providing hands-on online training in 3D design for primary and secondary school students around the country. Website: www.websitem.gazi.edu.tr/site/ahmetcelik

Mark Dorling's vision is to see all young people, across the world, have a quality computing education. Mark is a primary-trained teacher with many years of both primary and secondary teaching, teacher training, commercial educational training and industry experience. He is currently National CPD Coordinator with Computing At School (CAS) where he leads the Department for Education funded Master Teacher programme. Mark is leaving his role at CAS to pursue his passion, by moving closer to the classroom and studying for his PhD in Computing Education at Queen Mary University of London.

Eleanor Hoskins is a Senior Lecturer within the Faculty of Education at Manchester Metropolitan University. Previous to this role she taught for ten years in several primary and Early Years settings across two different L.As and gained experience as Science and Numeracy Subject Leaders as well as taking responsibilities for Assessment and SENCo. In addition, she has also gained experiences as a School Improvement Teacher for Manchester L.A, Assistant Head and Deputy Headteacher. Within her management role in school she contributed to the creation and organisation of a new, functioning, open plan foundation stage before other schools and settings had progressed to this level. Further expertise within Early Years Foundation Stage involved trialling new approaches to continuous provision learning and taking a proactive lead with children, parents and staff to ensure thorough transition for children between Early Years Foundation Stage into Key Stage 1. Her research interests lie in the field of Early Years science exploration and technology and she focussed upon these areas when completing her Master's degree dissertation and a recent chapter for an edited publication.

Maggie Morrissey has considerable experience of teaching within primary schools and is a primary science and technology specialist. She has worked in all areas of the primary sector from Early Years Foundation Stage to year six. She has managed a variety of subject areas during her career and has been instrumental in raising the standards of technology use within the schools that she has taught in. Maggie is currently completing her Computing in Education MA at Kings College London, and is in the process of researching how technology can support the teaching and learning of English to non-native English speakers whilst she is based in Moscow, Russia. She has also worked as a freelance training consultant receiving many positive comments about the courses and training that she has run. Further details can be found here www.technologytoteach.co.uk

Assoc. Prof. Dr. Selçuk Özdemir is married and has two daughters. He has been working on the development and use of educational software since his undergraduate years. His focus is especially on creating self learning environments where kids can gain skills in coding, 3D design, web design, robotic design/coding and entrepreneurship. He is the founder of Bilişim Garaj Akademisi (ICT Garage Academy) (bilisimgarajakademisi.com), where children aged 7-16 years can learn how to use computers and internet as a production and problem solving tool using online learning content. Website: www.w3.gazi.edu.tr/~sozdemir/index_eng.htm

Ellie Overland is the subject coordinator for PGCE in Computing with ICT at Manchester Metropolitan University. The outcomes for students on her course are exceptionally high and she has recently been nominated for an 'outstanding innovation in teaching' award. Ellie is also a highly experienced and effective leader of computing and ICT, she has experience of leading departments in inner-city schools across the Greater Manchester area. She is renowned for engaging pupils and rapidly raising standards and pupil progress. Having spent four years as a Local Authority consultant specialising in ICT, e-learning and 14-19 curriculum, Ellie has a broad knowledge base she uses to develop colleagues through CPD and classroom support. She has worked with numerous schools to develop classroom practice, plan for improvement and raise standards. Her current CPD offer supports teachers, both primary and secondary, in their subject knowledge for the Computing Curriculum and preparation to deliver both A Level and GCSE Computer Science. In addition, Ellie is studying for her EdD. Her research interests include curriculum change through CPD and teacher identity in computing education.

Sue Pope is an Academic Division Lead for STEM Education at Manchester Metropolitan University. For five years she was the national lead for mathematics 5-19 at the Qualifications and Curriculum Authority (QCA) where she managed and quality assured substantial research, development and evaluation projects. She coordinated QCA's work around STEM education. She moved to QCA after ten years in higher education working with beginning primary and secondary teachers on undergraduate and postgraduate courses, and supporting experienced teachers working towards higher degrees through researching their own practice and developing their knowledge and understanding of mathematics and its pedagogy. For a short time she worked as a local authority adviser. She taught for ten years in a number of schools, including five years as head of mathematics in an 11-18 mixed comprehensive school where she worked closely with feeder primary schools initiating strategies for enabling primary-secondary transition and cross-phase approaches to assessment. Sue is a long-standing active member of the Association of Teachers of Mathematics and currently chairs its General Council.

John Woollard first started teaching 'before computers' in the classroom but since 1978 has taught *about* and *with* computers in all phases including Early Years, primary, secondary, GCE, undergraduate and postgraduate. He is a teacher trainer working across the phases, author of psychology books, doctorate supervisor and assessor for computer science. He currently researches the teaching of computing, computer science and e-learning. John has been involved with several projects developing teaching resources and learning environments including CAS Barefoot for primary teaching and learning in virtual worlds.

Introduction

This book has been written for primary teacher trainees, in-service primary school teachers and teacher support staff to develop their knowledge and understanding of Primary Computing. The book is also useful for parents and teachers, from any country, to gain an insight into what young children learn, when working with different types of technology, from the Early Years Foundation Stage through to Key Stage 3.

Our book includes examples of activities to support you, as you develop your knowledge and skills, by introducing you to different and exciting aspects of technology, for example Web 2 tools, coding, film, animation and podcasting! We have included a separate chapter, which refers to e-safety and digital citizenship. We believe this guidance should be used to support all teaching and support staff in educational settings.

The book contains a chapter for supporting teachers and support staff in the Early Years Foundation Stage and also includes another chapter called 'Transition'. This has been included to support computing secondary school teachers, with the transition from the primary phase. Within both chapters, there are a wide range of innovative and creative activities, which will help to support all learners.

We are aware of the difficulties when planning and assessing computing, due to both the nature of the subject and the changes within the curriculum. Due to this, we have provided some examples to support your planning and assessment of computing, however, they should only be used as a guide, as we believe that every school will develop their own schemes, according to both their learners needs and the schools approach to their curriculum organization.

Although we have shared sample activities for different age groups, we have ensured these are flexible and can be taught in different age phases and be linked to a wide range of curriculum topics to suit your needs. The lesson sequences aim to help you model children's learning, through both plugged and unplugged activities, which provide opportunities for meeting the needs of both the learners, and also for ongoing assessment.

We are also aware that children learn about technology, not only during the computing sessions in the ICT suite, but across the curriculum. The increased use of tablets in education and recent focus on physical computing has also helped to make this possible. This requires different approaches to assessment. Using the suggested badge method, as part of your assessment criteria, will provide instant feedback for your children, and will help them to identify the skills and knowledge they have gained. This will help learners monitor their own learning and celebrate their achievement.

We would like to thank all of the authors who have contributed to this book and made it happen. We would also like to mention Susan Adams who provided the activity 3.2 Underwater fun for our book.

We hope that you will find this book useful and incorporate some of our suggested activities to create your own computing scheme. Happy computing!

Chapter 1

What is computing?

By Yasemin Allsop

COMPUTING PROGRAMME OF STUDY

'Computing' is the name of the subject that replaced ICT in the Primary National Curriculum (DfE, 2013). There is still confusion around what 'computing' actually means and what it consists of in relation to a student's learning. In this chapter we will explain computing in detail and then look at how to plan effective lessons to meet the requirements of the new Computing Curriculum.

We can analyse the new Computing Curriculum through three interrelated strands; computer science, information technology and digital literacy. We cannot assume that we teach these strands independently from each other, and they all are equally important as they all provide learners with functional skills that are crucial for their learning, both at school and outside of the school.

Computer science is basically the study of how computer systems work. This includes exploring how computers and computational processes work and how they are constructed and programmed. Computer scientists create algorithms to transform information and abstractions into model complex systems. The most important skill for a computer scientist is problem solving. Problem solving involves formulating problems, thinking creatively about solutions, and designing a clear solution. Teaching children to think like a computer scientist helps them to understand how computers think when solving problems, which in turn promotes computational thinking.

Based on the ability to think logically, algorithmically and recursively; **computational thinking** involves knowledge of the fundamentals of computing such as algorithms, abstraction, iteration, and generalisation. It also includes logical reasoning, problem decomposition, testing, debugging and visualisation skills. Developing these skills enables students, to represent and solve problems computationally in any discipline and daily life. Children develop these skills through designing algorithms and writing programs.

Information technology focuses on how computer applications can be used in a creative way to design solutions for a wide range of problems. Students learn about skills such as internet search techniques, evaluating the reliability of websites and basic email skills.

Digital literacy relates to using computer applications and systems effectively. Using 'office applications', using the internet and taking part in collaborative activities through social media and Web 2 tools are basic examples of this. It is vital that students explore the responsible use of technology. This helps students to become an active and responsible participant of the digital world.

Computing programme of study
As we briefly discussed above, in the new Computing Curriculum there is a strong focus on teaching children about how computer systems work, algorithms and writing programs. We are aware that there are many tools and programs available for teachers to teach the objectives of the new program of study, however, it is not possible to learn how to use these and implement this into every lesson. It is better to focus on the tools and programs that you are comfortable with, as long as you can use them to design activities to teach the skills and knowledge that are required in the Primary Computing Curriculum. Pages 13-17 provide information about what children should be taught in both Key Stages 1 and 2, along with some suggested activities and resources that can be used for teaching computing lessons.

Key Stage 1

1

CHILDREN SHOULD BE TAUGHT TO:

Understand what algorithms are, how they are implemented as programs on digital devices, and that programs execute by following a sequence of instructions

SUGGESTED ACTIVITIES

- You can provide indoor and outdoor opportunities for children to give and follow instructions *eg* making toast, route to school.
- You can ask children to work in pairs to carry out some instructions *eg* brushing teeth or setting directions in the classroom using Bee-Bots, roamers.

RESOURCES & USEFUL LINKS

Bee-Bots
Roamers
www.rethinkingict.wikispaces.com
Algorithms
www.martingsaunders.com/2013/03/
a-workshop-on-algorithms-for-primary-
schools/

RELEVANT CHAPTERS

3, 5, 6, 12

2

CHILDREN SHOULD BE TAUGHT TO:

Design, write and debug simple programs

SUGGESTED ACTIVITIES

- Retell a story using picture cards. Put the cards in the wrong order. Can they sequence the events correctly? You could lay the cards on the floor and use Bee-Bot to visit different events in a sequence.
- Model how to create a dance routine by creating a sequence of dance movements. Then show how to create the same dance routine using software such as Scratch.
- Provide them with problem solving tasks on Scratch, let them design solutions (See Chapter 3).

RESOURCES & USEFUL LINKS

Bee-Bots
Scratch
Story cards
www.scratch.mit.edu
www.incredibox.com

RELEVANT CHAPTERS

3, 8, 12

3

CHILDREN SHOULD BE TAUGHT TO:

Communicate safely and respectfully online, keeping personal information private, and recognise common uses of information technology beyond school

SUGGESTED ACTIVITIES

- Who should they talk to when someone or something upsets them online?
- What do they understand from 'keeping personal information private'? You could also discuss what kind of technologies they use at home; do they offer collaborative activities with other people? For example having an Xbox live account that allows you to play with players from around the world. Discussions around the age rating of the games and films are very useful.

RESOURCES & USEFUL LINKS

IWB
Tablets
PCs
Relevant videos
www.digital-literacy.org.uk

RELEVANT CHAPTERS

9, 10

4

CHILDREN SHOULD BE TAUGHT TO:

Use logical reasoning to predict the behaviour of simple programs

SUGGESTED ACTIVITIES

- Provide children with opportunities where they can predict the outcome of a set of instructions.
- Children talk about a set of instructions to move a Probot to draw shapes. They write it, test it and correct any errors. They then place their instructions in a box or bag without naming it. They select a random instruction sheet from the bag and try to identify the shape.
- You can also evaluate the instructions as a whole class. You could ask the children if the instructions were correct for their purpose? How can you make them better?
- This activity can also be done using LOGP, Scratch, Daisy the Dinosaur or Hopscotch. Children can write scripts to move objects and keep the outcome a secret. Their partners can try to guess the action/ effect on screen.

RESOURCES & USEFUL LINKS

Probot
Scratch
Hopscotch
Daisy the Dinosaur
www.iboard.co.uk/iwb/
Drawing-with-a-Control-Toy-697
aspx?topic=6&resource=8

RELEVANT CHAPTERS

3, 5, 8, 12

5

CHILDREN SHOULD BE TAUGHT TO:

Organise, store, manipulate and retrieve data in a range of digital formats

SUGGESTED ACTIVITIES

- Using a PBL (Project Based Learning) approach and teaching within a context will make learning more relevant to learners. Providing opportunities for children to learn in a context such as story-telling using a stop-motion animation or creating a presentation on a specific topic over a longer period of time will enable them to master many transferable skills including collaboration, communication, creativity, and critical thinking. Let the children create documents using either a word-processor or online Web 2 tools such as Wikis. They should practice writing sentences, insert images/ clip art, correcting their mistakes.

RESOURCES & USEFUL LINKS

Wikis
Blogs
Word processing software
Animation software
www.clayanimator.com/english/stop_
motion_animator.html
http://connectingclassroomswithchina.
wikispaces.com
Wilbury+Primary+School
http://kidblog.org/home/
www.abcya.com/animate.htm

RELEVANT CHAPTERS

2, 6, 7, 8, 10

1

CHILDREN SHOULD BE TAUGHT TO:

Design, write and debug programs that accomplish specific goals, including controlling or simulating physical systems; solve problems by decomposing them into smaller parts

SUGGESTED ACTIVITIES

- It is always useful to start with algorithm games to remind children of the importance of having precise instructions in the correct order to achieve specific goals *eg* maze games are brilliant for developing the use of directional language and creating sequences.
- Hopscotch, Scratch and Alice 2.3 can be used by children to design simple games such as; racing where they can develop their programming skills.
- Programs such as Enchanting can be used with Scratch for children to write programs to control physical objects. You can view an example below: www.youtube.com/watch?v=dXdCoynhsBs

RESOURCES & USEFUL LINKS

Scratch
Alice 2.3
Tynker
Hopscotch
Machineers
Lego We Do
www.tesconnect.com/scratch-curriculum
www.games.thinkingmyself.com

RELEVANT CHAPTERS

3, 5, 8, 12

2

CHILDREN SHOULD BE TAUGHT TO:

Understand computer networks including the internet; how they can provide multiple services, such as the world wide web; and the opportunities they offer for communication and collaboration

SUGGESTED ACTIVITIES

- Tell the children to get in a circle and put one hand on the shoulder of the person standing next to them. Say a sentence to one of the children and ask her/him to pass it on to the next child. Can the message be passed correctly, or are any parts missing in the process? What happens if one child removes their hand from the shoulder of another? Can the message still be carried around?
- Discuss with the children how computers from all around the world understand each other (They use the same language – TCP/IP). Watch the videos listed right with children and let them ask questions or just share their thoughts. You could also ask the children to draw a diagram of how the internet works before and after the lesson to check their understanding.
- Ask how email messages work, how our messages are transported to another recipient? Watch the following video with children and then re-think the answers for the previous question. www.ictvideohelp.co.uk/internet/internetpackages/internetpackages.html

RESOURCES & USEFUL LINKS

Relevant videos
Mind mapping software
www.thekidshouldseethis.com/post/26674356049
www.youtube.com/watch?v=7_LPdttKXPc
www.youtube.com/watch?v=C3sr7_0FyPA

RELEVANT CHAPTERS

3

3

CHILDREN SHOULD BE TAUGHT TO:

Use sequence, selection, and repetition in programs; work with variables and various forms of input and output; generate appropriate inputs and predicted outputs to test programs

SUGGESTED ACTIVITIES

- Probot can be used for practising sequencing and repetitions. Children can discuss how many times an instruction needs to be repeated for example to draw a rectangle. A similar activity can also be done using Scratch.
- Simple maze games on Scratch can be used to model repetition and loops.
- Discuss with children the elements of a game. You can compare a Scratch animation and Scratch game. Focus on time, score, levels *etc*. These are variables. Allow the children to design their own game using loops and variables. You can use this template to help them with their planning.

RESOURCES & USEFUL LINKS

Scratch
Probot
Alice 2.3
https://blockly-demo.appspot.com/static/apps/maze/index.html?lang=en
http://www.bbc.co.uk/guides/zqrq7ty
www.code-it.co.uk/year4/scratchspidermaze2.pdf
https://slp.somerset.gov.uk/cypd/elim/somersetict/Site%20Pages/Scratch.aspx

RELEVANT CHAPTERS

3, 5, 8, 12

4

CHILDREN SHOULD BE TAUGHT TO:

Use logical reasoning to explain how some simple algorithms work and to detect and correct errors in algorithms and programs

SUGGESTED ACTIVITIES

- Use the activities at www.games.thinkingmyself.com to introduce algorithms.
- Give examples of algorithms from daily lives. Examples can be seen at: www.ehow.com/info_8394031_kinds-everyday-algorithms.html.
- Ask students to create an algorithm to tell a simple story or joke using Scratch or Alice.
- Ask students to write a sequence of instructions for a car racing game then exchange them with their friends. Students can sequence their friends pre-written lines of programming into order and identify any problems.
- Use the A.L.E.X app and Cargo-Bot to encourage children to talk about the algorithm that will be required to meet the higher levels of challenge.

RESOURCES & USEFUL LINKS

Scratch
Alice 2.3
A.L.E.X
Cargo-Bot
www.tesconnect.com/algorithm
http://code.google.com/p/blockly/
https://itunes.apple.com/gb/app/i-logo/id435280247?mt=8
www.fmslogo.sourceforge.net

RELEVANT CHAPTERS

3, 5, 8, 12

5

CHILDREN SHOULD BE TAUGHT TO:

Describe how internet search engines find and store data; use search engines effectively; be discerning in evaluating digital content; respect individuals and intellectual property; use technology responsibly, securely and safely

SUGGESTED ACTIVITIES

- Look at 'How search engines work' (Link 2) infographic with children. Discuss the key words such as crawlers, ranking, database. Can they come up with methods that will help them to find what they are looking for effectively? How do they check to see if the information they have found is real.
- Ask the children to design a poster to present useful strategies that they need for searching on the internet.
- Discuss fair use and copyright with the children. Use the Cyberbee website to check their understanding.
- Use the www.digital-literacy.org.uk website to teach children about internet safety, cyberbullying, privacy, digital footprints and information literacy.

RESOURCES & USEFUL LINKS

Internet access
Materials for poster design or software
www.kidsdiscover.com/infographics/
infographic-how-search-engines-work/
www.abbotswood.hants.sch.uk/
planning/internet-research-skills.htm
www.cyberbee.com/cb_copyright.swf
www.commonsensemedia.org/
educators/lesson/copyrights-and-
wrongs

RELEVANT CHAPTERS

8, 9

6

CHILDREN SHOULD BE TAUGHT TO:

Select, use and combine a variety of software (including internet services) on a range of digital devices to accomplish given goals, including collecting, analyzing, evaluating and presenting data and information

SUGGESTED ACTIVITIES

This strand of the Computing Curriculum can be taught through cross-curricular activities. Provide opportunities for children to:
- Use different online tools, software and hardware to achieve specific goals
- To review, edit, share and evaluate their work
- Work collaboratively and independently

Example activities:

- Using programs and apps like Keynote, PowerPoint, Prezi, Book creator app to create presentations.
- Use Padlet, Primary Pad or similar online tools to create and share ideas collaboratively.
- Creating animations, podcasts or films to share and evaluate their ideas.

RESOURCES & USEFUL LINKS

Data handling software
Presentation software
Relevant Web 2 tools
www.padlet.com
www.prezi.com/profile/
registration/?license_type=PUBLIC
www.launchpadtoys.com/toontastic/
www.primarypad.com
www.ictinpractice.com/wp-content/
uploads/2013/06/web-2-tools-2013.pdf

RELEVANT CHAPTERS

2, 4, 5, 6, 7, 9

Planning and teaching effective computing lessons

When planning and teaching computing lessons there are some important elements that should be considered. It is important to remember that how good our teaching will be, depends on how well the lesson was planned. We need to make sure that we look at each learning situation individually and structure our activities to meet the needs of our learners. This includes supporting not just those who need extra support to complete their tasks and meet their objectives but also for those who exceed their targets and will benefit from undertaking extended learning opportunities. Below is some brief information about some principles that we should follow when planning and teaching effective computing lessons.

Having a secure subject knowledge, not just of what has been taught, but also of the tools used is vital. Experimenting with the tools that will be used during the sessions, just like children, will help teachers to understand the thinking and learning process that children go through and identify any issues or misconceptions in advance.

Being aware of pedagogical approaches that work well in different situations especially when learning with, through and about technology will support teachers to adopt appropriate teaching strategies. This will also be useful for teachers to analyse the role of the learners and how this relates to the role of the teachers as learning will be shaped through the students' interaction with their peers, tools and teachers. For example, especially when teaching coding, there will be times where the teacher won't have one straightforward answer, but will explore different solutions collaboratively with students. This two-way interaction between learners and teachers can be defined as a **co-learning** experience.

Designing learning experiences that provide opportunities for learners to develop and apply transferable skills such as problem solving, creativity, communication, critical thinking, collaborative work and technology skills. These skills can aid the process of developing deeper learning that can prepare students for more complex learning situations and their future life.

Adopting a flexible learning space approach for children to be able to move around and discuss their works with their peers. After many years observing children during technology lessons, we found that they enjoy talking about their work and finding out what others are doing. It is important to allow the children to move around and discuss their friend's work, make suggestions or ask for help. This would help the students to feel comfortable within the learning space, rather than being restricted which can be very motivational. It would also help them to evaluate both theirs and their friends' work, which would help them to monitor their own learning.

Focusing on cross-curricular learning where possible. Planning and teaching computing in a context that is relevant to the children's learning in other subjects will make learning more engaging and memorable. It is useful to create a cross-curricular idea map to help you with planning. The table opposite shows some example ideas of a cross-curricular teaching approach to computing.

Ensuring that **health and safety regulations** are followed. When using tablets in class and other physical systems that may require a different arrangement and management of the classroom. For example we need to consider issues when plugging Raspberry Pi's or Makey Makey's or any other tools and how we would handle them.

E-safety issues and how these would be integrated into a lesson need to be clearly identified. We believe that e-safety should be included in every lesson to emphasise the specific concerns related to the topic studied. If children are learning about blogs then online safety can be discussed as part of the session so that children will remember it when they work on their blog. Teaching about the dangers of the internet and how to manage its risks in a context will help students to learn to use technology in a responsible way.

Ancient worlds	Mathematics
Class Wiki on Wikispaces for children to keep record of their research and work on ancient civilisations	Using Logo and Scratch to draw 2D shapes
Designing an Egyptian village in Minecraft	Using floor robots to create 2D shapes
News reports about daily life during Roman Britain	Comparing Denary and Binary numbers, investigating place value
Telling a story about Egypt using Scratch or Alice 2.3	Using floor robots to teach about reading coordinates
Form governments to guide your citizens in Civilisation game	Position and direction; teaching children about directional language and angles through unplugged computing activities and floor robots
Running blogs using Kidblogs could be on any aspects of the ancient worlds	Constructing charts, pictograms and graphs
Creating a documentary about Romans/Egyptians/Greeks using green screen filming tools	Using spreadsheets to complete calculations and solve problems
Science	**Literacy**
Observe/record/monitor using data logger, digital camera or an app Changes in weather/seasons, local environment and materials	Digital story telling using apps and programs
	Using Wikis for collaborative writing
Sorting/Grouping using a software Plants Animals Materials	Blogs for both independent and collaborative writing activities
	Creating books using apps or web based applications such as Storybird
Simulations Solar system Electrical circuits	Designing a newspaper using different programs such as Word, Publisher or Pages
	Creating a news report, adverts or a radio show using video or podcasting
Research skills, using online sources to find out about: Living things and their habitat, parts of animals and the human body	Using films in education to engage learners with speaking and writing activities

Table 1: Suggested cross-curricular teaching ideas for computing

Chapter 2

Computing in the Early Years

By Eleanor Hoskins

About this chapter

In this chapter, technology within Early Years education is explored. Three activities are outlined to develop young children's learning and understanding with basic technology. The activities help young children use technology to explore the world around them and are designed to enhance and enthuse their young minds.

Firm foundations for children's understanding, confidence and enthusiasm with future Primary Computing need to be carefully laid within Early Years to allow children to begin their essential educational journey within this area.

ACTIVITIES

1. Hide and Seek
2. I Spy
3. Park Adventure

CROSS-CURRICULAR

The activities have cross- curricular/cross-area 'prime' and 'specific' statutory framework for the Early Years Foundation Stage (2012) links as follows:

- The 'Hide and Seek' activity with iPad's combines 'prime areas' of communication and language; understanding through following instructions, physical development (moving and handling- control and coordination) with the 'specific areas' of technology, literacy (reading and understanding simple sentences) and understanding the world.

- The 'I Spy' activity using Easi-Scope's joins 'prime areas' of physical development (moving and handling- control and coordination) and personal social and emotional development (managing feelings and behaviour – working in pairs) with the 'specific areas' of technology, understanding the world (The world – observing plants) and expressive arts and design (Being imaginative – exploring drawing).

- 'Park Adventure' with a Bee-Bot links 'prime areas' of communication and language (Listening and attention – understanding-following instructions) and Physical Development (Moving and handling- control and coordination of movement) with 'Specific Areas' of Technology, Mathematics (Numbers-counting and Shape, space and measures – position and distance) and Understanding the world (The world – environments).

USEFUL LINKS

www.qrstuff.com

www.youtube.com/watch?v=Y-lD5_ZCuy8

2.1 Hide and Seek

INTRODUCTION

In this activity the children will learn how to use QR coding to support a minibeast hunt. **QR (Quick Response codes),** allow children to access a chosen website or other data quickly and safely. In addition, the ease of the 'point and go' approach fits with young children's limited attention spans and allows a harmonious approach to cross-area learning unfold.

TEACHING SEQUENCE

➡ In preparation for this activity QR codes will need to be generated and printed for chosen minibeast images or websites, using a QR code generator. iPads or other tablets will also need to be ready with a QR code reader app installed. Lastly, a small trail outside with printed QR codes displayed at various habitat locations will need to be set up. Number each QR code so the children can follow in sequence.

Introduction

➡ To build upon previous learning about minibeasts and habitats in the world around us, children need to recap over key creatures such as woodlice, spiders, snails and worms.

➡ Focus upon the physical characteristics of what each minibeast looks like and ask the children to draw pictures of each minibeast and share ideas. What do we know about these minibeasts? Can we play hide and seek and find out something about each minibeast?

➡ Explain to the children that they will go outside to play 'hide and seek' with the minibeasts. Following a trail in small groups they will 'seek out' chosen minibeasts in their different habitats to find out something about them.

Learning Objective
- Select and use technology for a particular purpose

Key Vocabulary
- QR code
- QR code image
- Screen

Resources
- Tablets (with QR code reader installed)
- Printed QR codes

Explore and Play

➡ Introduce the children to a printed QR code and discuss what it looks like. Explain how the codes can be used to find out information. Model with the children how to select a QR code reader app and how to point the tablet screen at the QR code using the camera image so the children can see the transition to a chosen page.

➡ Allow the children to have a five-minute 'explore and play' in pairs to try selecting the QR code reader app and pointing the tablet at a QR code to access information.

Application Activity

➡ After the 'explore and play' time the children should go outside in groups of five with an adult and a tablet each to follow the minibeast trail.

➡ As the children move around the trail (in numbered sequence) they should be encouraged by the accompanying adult to observe the habitat, seek out any minibeasts that live there and then scan the appropriate QR code to access information.

➡ Each QR code should take the children to a simple website, image, video or pre saved text about the minibeasts. Once accessing the chosen information, the children should be encouraged to look at photos, illustrations, simple sentences and then listen as the group adult reads a small amount of the information out loud.

➡ This process should be repeated for each minibeast and QR code location so the group of children can retrieve simple information about each minibeast.

ROUND UP!

As each group of children return from their minibeast trail, they should immediately share something they have learnt about each minibeast. The shared information should then be recorded and collated on either an interactive whiteboard or poster to revisit as a whole group later or the next day.

ASSESSMENT OPPORTUNITIES

Whilst the children are exploring during the minibeasts trail, the supervising adult should take photographs of children accessing the QR codes and make notes of any interesting comments on post-it notes.

REPETITION AND CONSOLIDATION

Young children need the opportunity to repeat the process of following and accessing QR codes in different contexts to retrieve varied information and cement their understanding about how to use QR coding in context. Different approaches for this could include:

✓ Materials hunt
✓ Flowers trail
✓ Tree discovery

2.2 I Spy

INTRODUCTION

In this activity the children will learn how to develop their observational skills with the help of technology. They will be introduced to Easi-Scopes, which are hand held, digital, USB microscopes that magnify and capture images for young children to clearly observe.

TEACHING SEQUENCE

In preparation for this activity, flowers will need to be purchased and prepared. The best preparation means the flowers should be individually cut approximately 10cm below the flower head.

TIP: look for bunches of mixed flowers so children can access a variety of different flower shapes and patterns

Introduction

➡ Begin by building upon any previous learning about flowers. Where do we see flowers? Are all flowers the same? Hand out different, individual flowers to pairs of children to observe, touch, smell and talk about.

➡ Recap over key flower parts: petal, leaf, stem.

Explore and Play

➡ Introduce the Easi-Scopes and model how to use. Connect to an interactive whiteboard and model to the children *how* to focus upon an image by turning the dial at the top and *how* to capture an image by clicking the button on top. Discuss how clearly we can see the flower parts using the digital microscope.

➡ Allow the children five minutes to work in pairs to 'explore and play' with the Easi-

Learning Objective
- Select and use technology for a particular purpose
- Recognise technology used in school

Key Vocabulary
- Easi-Scope
- Laptop
- Click
- Turn

Resources
- Easi-Scopes
- Laptops
- Flowers
- Plastic tweezers

Scopes attached to laptops and a flower. Encourage and guide the children to use the dial to focus as well as clicking to capture an image. Focus the children's attention upon the captured image then displayed on the laptop.

Application Activity

➡ Following the 'explore and play' time explain to the children they will play 'I Spy' with a flower and use the Easi-Scope to help them look very carefully. After spying very carefully they can draw what they see. Remind the children to look at the petal shape, size, colour and model how to use plastic tweezers to pull petals to look inside.

➡ Arrange the children paired within a small group, each pair with a flower, laptop and Easi-Scope. An accompanying adult must sit with the children to ensure they look carefully and operate the Easi-Scope as guided.

➡ If the children are struggling to draw an image from viewing alone, an accompanying adult must encourage the children to capture an image onto the laptop and then draw a simple image from this.

As a whole group return to the carpet space after all children have had a turn to complete the observation activity. Some images captured from today can be displayed through the interactive whiteboard. Recap over key vocabulary introduced during the introduction (petal, leaf, and stem) and discuss, whilst looking at images, these features. Also discuss the different colours and shapes that can be seen using the digital microscope.

ASSESSMENT OPPORTUNITIES
Whilst the children are exploring the use of the Easi-Scope there should be lots of opportunities to capture the application of their understanding and skills. The images that some children capture using the Easi-Scopes can be stored with accompanying observational notes

REPETITION AND CONSOLIDATION
Young children need the opportunity to repeat the process of observing clearly using the Easi-Scope. They should practice to ensure they are able to focus and capture images with ease.

2.3 Park Adventure

INTRODUCTION

In this activity the children will learn how to operate a simple floor robot to move forwards and backwards. The operation of the Bee-Bot will support their learning in mathematics alongside physical development focusing upon manipulation and control of an object.

TEACHING SEQUENCE

In preparation for this activity ensure the Bee-Bot floor robot is fully charged. It would also be useful to have created a park floor map with the children in preparation to ensure this activity can focus upon programming the floor robot alone.

Park floor map: On poster paper create a floor map with the children of a park. Encourage the children to create four pathways (straight lines of different lengths) leading to different areas *eg* slide, swings, pond, and roundabout.

TIP: If you wish to make a textured map then a transparent grid cover can be purchased to act as an overlay to allow the floor robot to still travel over the surface.

Learning Objective
- Select and use technology for a particular purpose
- Recognise technology used in school

Key Vocabulary
- Forwards
- Backwards
- GO

Resources
- Floor robot (Bee-Bot)
- Floor map (pre constructed)
- Cards
- Park 'visit cards'

Introduction

➡ Recap over the park floor map already created. Introduce Bee-Bot the floor robot and talk about what he looks like. Explain that Bee-Bot likes to follow instructions and that it will be following their instructions along the park map today.

➡ Introduce the control buttons on Bee-Bot. Look at the different symbols and discuss.

➡ Focus on the forward ↑ and backward ↓ buttons. What are these directions? Ask the children to stand up and practice moving forwards and backwards. Use ↑ and ↓ cards and practice holding up the cards so the children can move forwards or backwards in response.

➡ Model using arrow cards with a stated number *eg* hold up ↑ and say '3' to model moving forwards 1,2,3 steps. Ask the children to try this whilst forwards and backwards direction cards are held up and numbers are stated. Guide the children with the steady counting.

➡ Return to the Bee-Bot floor robot and focus back on the forward and backward arrow buttons. Model how the forwards or backwards arrows can be pressed different times to move the floor robot different distances. Also, show how the floor robot's 'Go' button must be pressed to begin its movements.

➡ Contrast how far the Bee-Bot floor robot moves when the forwards or backwards arrows are pressed *once* in comparison to *five* times.

Explore and Play

➡ Allow the children five minutes to work in pairs to explore and play with the Bee-Bot floor robot. Encourage the children to explore operating the forwards and backwards arrows.
NB: how this is organized will depend on how many Bee-Bots are available.

➡ Pause the children to model how the 'clear' button can be pressed before starting a new movement.
Allow the children another two minutes exploration using the 'clear' button.

Application Activity

➡ Explain how Bee-Bot is going to explore their park map today and would like to visit all areas.

➡ Work with children in groups of three to operate Bee-Bot around the map. Ask children to take it in turns to choose a 'visit card'. Each visit card will display a photo, illustration or word for destinations; swings, slide, roundabout, and pond. The visit cards should match exactly to chosen destinations on the created map.

➡ The children will then work as a team, supported by an adult, to programme Bee-Bot to move along the map and reach the destination specified on the visit card. The adult should support the children to carefully count out loud whilst they press the correct directional buttons.

➡ Repeat the above activity until all children have had an opportunity to choose a destination visit card and programme Bee-Bot.

ROUND UP!

➡ After all children have had turns to work with the floor robot in very small, guided groups, gather all children to sit back on the carpet as a large group. Recap over how the forwards and backwards, Go and clear buttons can be used.

➡ Explain that Bee-Bot has enjoyed his time so much that it would like to now have a dance! Ask different children to help programme some continuous forwards and backwards directions and then press GO at the same time as music is played!

ASSESSMENT OPPORTUNITIES

Whilst the children are exploring how to operate the floor robot there should be lots of opportunities to capture learning through photographs and videos. Short video clips or photos with accompanying observational notes can then be stored for chosen children.

REPETITION AND CONSOLIDATION

Young children need the opportunity to repeat the process of programming and operating a floor robot. They should practice to ensure they are able to programme with ease.

The next step is to teach children how to programme turns but this must not be started until the children have a firm understanding of programming and operating forwards and backwards movements of different lengths.

The use of floor maps provides good opportunities to practice operating the floor robot through different movements.

Different maps can be created of a:
✓ beach
✓ zoo
✓ farm

REFERENCES

Johnston, J. (2005) *Early Explorations in Science.* 2nd ed. , Berkshire: Open University Press

Siraj-Blatchford, J. And Whitebread, D. (2003) *Supporting Information and Communications Technology in the Early Years.* Buckingham: Open University Press

Whitebread, D. (2008) Introduction; young children learning and early years teaching In: Whitebread, D., Coltman, P. (eds.) *Teaching and learning in the early years.* 3rd ed. Oxon. Routledge.

Chapter 3

Tell a story and make a game

By Yasemin Allsop

About this chapter

In this chapter children will learn about programming concepts such as **sequence**, **loop, conditionals** and **variables** through story telling and making games using freely available programs and apps. They will complete sequences of plugged and unplugged tasks, which can be modified to meet the needs of children in both Key Stage 1 and Key Stage 2. Children will experience using the ScratchJr app and Scratch programming environment. They will be actively involved in either self-assessment or peer assessment to monitor their own learning progress.

KEY TERMS

Algorithm: a set of precise instructions to solve a problem or achieve a goal.

Sequence: a set of events or instructions that must be carried out in a specific order within an algorithm.

Selection: Selection is all about decision making, which comes as an outcome of asking questions.

Debugging: Identifying and removing errors from scripts and programs.

Variable: a value, which can change depending on conditions. Variables are used for holding on to a value to use later.

Loops: a sequence of instructions that are repeated until a specific task is achieved.

Conditionals: an instruction in a program that is only executed when a specific condition is met.

ACTIVITIES

1. Tell me your story!
2. 2D shapes: What shape am I?
3. Underwater fun
4. Make Hopping frog game

CROSS-CURRICULAR

- Tell me your story could be embedded into literacy lessons. Children can plan their story before telling it using the Scratch program.

- 2D shapes activity provide opportunities for children to learn about the properties of 2D shapes and Scratch programming environment.

- The Hopping frog game is a fun way of learning about habitats of animals. This activity can be linked to science.

USEFUL LINKS

www.scratch.mit.edu

www.j2e.com/j2code/

www.ictinpractice.com/a-big-list-of-apps-programs-and-websites-for-teaching-coding-and-game-design/

3.1 Tell me your story!

INTRODUCTION

This activity will provide opportunities for children to experiment with Scratch programming environment before they move onto more complex projects. Children will discuss their favourite stories with their peers and then create a storyboard collaboratively in pairs or groups. They will explore Scratch program and plan how they could create their story using Scratch codes. Although this is a story telling activity, using Scratch as a tool to present ideas will help children to learn about 'algorithms', 'repetition', 'loop', 'selection', 'sequence' and 'debugging'. Children can share their completed stories and evaluate it to make it better.

TEACHING SEQUENCE

➡ Ask children about their favourite stories. Let them share their favourite stories in pairs. Get feedback.

➡ Discuss with children points such as; what makes a good story, how to structure a story, what functions should be used to create a story in Scratch. Use these points to create an evaluation sheet with them.

➡ Explain to children that they will be telling a story using Scratch program. Let them visit https://scratch.mit.edu/explore/projects/stories/ to look at some examples of stories created in Scratch.

➡ Model how to use Scratch for telling simple stories *eg* adding a sprite and a background, drawing a sprite and background, moving-gliding characters, changing costume, changing appearance, using 'say' block for conversation.

Learning Objective
- Use sequence, selection and repeat in programs
- Design and write programs that accomplish specific goals

Key Vocabulary
- Sequence
- Algorithm
- Selection
- Loop
- Debug

Resources
- Access to Scratch website
- Scratch stories' template

➡ Provide the students with Scratch Stories template and let them plan their stories in pairs. Make sure they keep a record of the changes they made on their design by writing it down on their planning sheet.

ROUND UP!

Give children time to create their story using the Scratch application. Once they have finished encourage them to share their story in the Scratch Gallery. Look at some of their stories as a whole class and talk about how to make it better.

Scratch Stories

Plan, create and share your story!

SCENE 1	**SCENE 2**
SCENE 3	**SCENE 4**

The story is about:

The first characters are:

What happens next?

How did the story end?

3.2 2D shapes: What shape am I?

INTRODUCTION

There are many coding programs that enable users to draw shapes, letters and patterns such as Logo, Scratch and Hopscotch. This provides a great opportunity to teach mathematics and computer science concepts at the same time through cross-curricular tasks. The Scratch pen function works in a very similar to a pencil. If you keep it down it leaves a trial line behind it, if you keep it up it doesn't. In this session children will learn to use the Scratch pen function to draw 2D shapes. For this they need to know about the properties of the shapes but also **sequence** of script that will draw specific shapes.

TEACHING SEQUENCE

➡ Play 'guess a shape' game with the children. Get one child to list the properties of a 2D shape and the rest of class try to name the shape.

➡ Discuss different types of angles of how far do you turn to make 90 degrees, 180 degrees, 60 degrees *etc*.

➡ **Walking shapes** Ask a child to stand up and repeat this instruction four times: Walk three steps, turn right 90 degrees. Ask the class to identify the shape. Discuss what helped them to decide. Ask another child to repeat the instructions again, this time while holding a chalk or a pen down on a large piece of paper. Did they identify the shape correctly?

➡ Create the same instructions using Scratch pen functions. Model how to draw a square. See overleaf.

➡ Explain to the children that some of the codes used when drawing a square are repetitive and they could use a repeat loop to create a shorter code to do the same task. Allow them time to try and work out the repeat loop. Let

Learning Objective
- Use sequence, selection and repeat in programs
- Design and write programs that accomplish specific goals
- Sort, describe and name 2D shapes

Key Vocabulary
- Sequence
- Algorithm
- Selection
- Loop
- Debug

Resources
- Access to Scratch website
- Scratch Stories' template

them share and explain their answers.

➡ Write properties of different 2D shapes on small post sticks. Put them inside a box. Children select a post stick, read the properties of the shapes, identify the shape and come up with a code to draw the shape using 'Pen' in Scratch. Their final task is to complete the 'Shape Challenges' sheet.

ROUND UP!

In plenary discuss the problems children had when working on shape challenges and the strategies they used to solve the problems.

Drawing a square using pen function

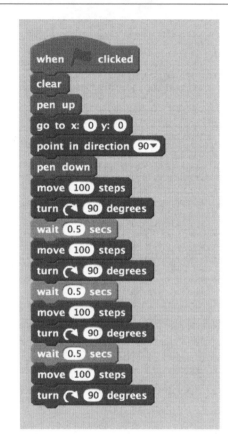

By putting 'wait' block in between loops, we allow children to see the process of drawing the shapes, otherwise they won't be able to see the turns.

USING THE REPEAT LOOP TO DRAW A SQUARE

3.2 SHAPE CHALLENGES

Can you write a loop to draw a triangle?

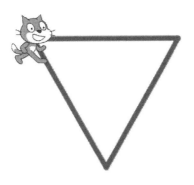

Look at the steps below to draw an octagon. Octagon is an eight sided shape. Can you fill in the blanks to make this loop work?

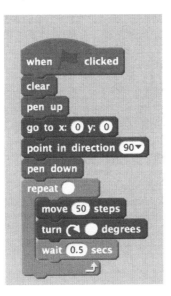

Can you write down the steps for drawing a simple house?

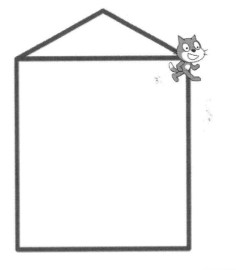

3.3 Tell a story: Underwater fun!

This activity has been contributed by Susan Adams

INTRODUCTION

In this activity the students will create their own underwater scene which will help them begin to understand how they can use computers to make things happen. Using ScratchJr they will create short algorithms for each character that they add to their scene. Children will use sequence and begin working towards loops by using the repeat forever function. This activity will introduce many functions available within ScratchJr, providing children with the skills to be able to explore and make their own scenes. As an extension the students will be challenged to adjust and debug the algorithms and to create their own algorithms.

TEACHING SEQUENCE

Introduce children to the term **algorithm** explain that an algorithm is a **sequence of precise instructions**. Explain that all digital devices need algorithms to make them work without them they will not do anything. Discuss algorithms that humans use in daily routines, *eg* when a teacher is talking, children apply the 'listening to teacher' algorithm. Break down each instruction that children apply and discuss the algorithm that they would use if the teacher asked a question. Be pedantic, children may forget to include putting their hands back down once the teacher has invited them to speak. Encourage children to provide examples of other daily algorithms that they use, children usually come up with getting up, eating, getting dressed, brushing teeth *etc* Explain that we can collect algorithms together to solve a larger problem *eg* getting to school. Discuss the importance of **sequence** within an algorithm.

➡ Tell the students that they will be creating an underwater animated scene using the

Learning Objective
- To create simple programs using simple drag and drop code
- Use sequence and repeat in programs

Key Vocabulary
- Algorithm
- Command
- Sequence
- Repeat
- Loop
- Debug

Resources
- ScratchJr Program on iPads
- Instruction sheet

ScratchJr program. Show them **Figure 3.3.1** and discuss what commands we might use to move each character.

➡ Provide the students with the 'underwater fun' instruction sheet overleaf. Let them complete the activity in pairs or independently. Remind the students to take either a screenshot or photo of the problems they may meet and keep a record of the strategies they used to solve them.

➡ When drawing a repetitive shape like a square encourage the children to use a

repeat loop to create a shorter code to do the same task. Give them time to work our and test the repeat loop. Let them share and explain their answers.

Figure 3.3.1: Underwater Fun Animation

ROUND UP!
Ask the class to share any problems they had when creating their underwater scenes and the strategies that they used to **debug** them. Select a student who attempted the challenges and adjusted the algorithms to change what a character did. Ask the student to explain how they adjusted the algorithm and what effect it had. Select a student who added more characters as a challenge and ask them to explain how they animated their new characters. Discuss what else can be done to make this animation more interesting.

ASSESSMENT OPPORTUNITIES
- You can ask the children to either film or take screenshots of their problem solving activites.
- They can annotate their completed work to explain how they designed their programs.

3.3 Underwater fun

STEP 1
Start a new ScratchJr project
Set the background:
Tap ![] to see the library.

Tap ![] to select the Underwater scene

Tap on the tick
Delete the cat:
Tap and hold the cat
Click on the ⊗ to remove the cat

STEP 2: Add in a swimming fish and diver
Tap ⊕ to add in a fish that swims when you touch it:
- Add a block to start the actions when you touch the fish
- Add a motion block to make your fish move right
- Add the repeat forever block so that your fish keeps moving

Add in a diver that looks like you and swims when you touch it:
- Tap 🔧 next to the diver. Select the camera, then select the blank divers face so that you can take your photo and add in your face.
- Add blocks to make your diver move right when you touch it.

STEP 3: Add a wiggly fish
Add in another different fish that moves when you touch it. Make your new fish look like it's swimming with a wiggle:
- Add a block to make your fish move right
- Add a block to make your fish turn right
- Add a block to make your fish move right
- Add a block to make your fish turn left
- Add the repeat forever block

STEP 4: Make a rock
- Tap ⊕ then click the paintbrush 🖌
- Select the thick paintbrush tool and choose a colour
- Make your rock shape

Extra: Choose another colour to add texture
- Click the tick

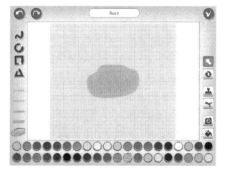

STEP 5: Add the crab and create its script
Add a crab, then make it hide behind the rock when touched:

- First move the rock to the bottom left corner over the dark hole
- Next move the crab beside the rock

- To make the crab look like it's moving backwards we will shrink it
- Next we need to make it move towards the rock for three moves, by tapping the number below and changing it

After our crab has hidden, it will need to come back again:

- The crab will need to move back to where it started, so move it in the opposite direction by three
- Make it grow again, to make it look like it is moving forward

Last, we need to make the crab wait before it runs away again:

- Drag the wait block to your script, just before repeat forever block

STEP 6: Add instructions

- We need to tell players how to make the characters move. Add a motion block to make your fish move right
- Click on 🌀 at the top of the screen

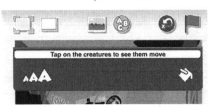

- Add your instructions

Test your game.

CHALLENGE!
Challenge 1:
Make the wiggly fish swim smoothly.
Challenge 2:
Make the diver say something.
Challenge 3:
Make a character move when you tap the green flag.
Challenge 4:
Make a change so that the crab only hides once when you touch it and doesn't keep hiding.
Challenge 5:
Add in the starfish and the seahorse. What will you make them do?

TIME TO CHECK AND DISCUSS
What problems did we have and how did we fix them?
- Who found that the crab not behind the rock?
- How did you fix this?

How can we make the crab hide for longer behind the rock?
Can you make the diver say something?
- What happens when we tap the diver?
- How can we correct this without using more blocks?

3.4 Make a game: Hopping frog!

INTRODUCTION

In this activity the students will make their first computer game called Hopping frog using Scratch. They will learn to use **sequence, selection, loop** and **variables** in the Scratch programming environment. As an extension the students will be challenged to create and use 'score' variable. If any children are not familiar with Scratch they must complete Activity 3 before starting this task. Tell children that when they complete making their game they will receive a 'computer master 1' badge for their assessment log. Those who complete the challenge task and create a score variable will also receive a 'super computer' badge.

TEACHING SEQUENCE

➡ Create a maze on the floor using tissue paper in a large indoor or outside space. Blindfold a child and move them to the starting point of the maze. Ask the other children to stand at the side of the maze and give them precise instructions to help the blindfolded student complete the maze. Encourage them to use positional language and mathematical vocabulary when giving instructions. Discuss how the **repeat** and **sequence** functions can be used to design an efficient solution. Repeat the activity a few times by changing the maze design. If needed let the children use a whiteboard to write down their instructions.

➡ Tell the students that they will be creating a game called Hopping frog using the Scratch program. Show them Figure 3.4.1 which outlines the Hopping frog game and discuss what script is needed to create each action.

➡ Provide the students with the Hopping frog instruction sheet. Let them complete the game either in pairs or independently. Remind the students to take either a screenshot or photo of the problems they may meet and keep a record of the strategies they used to solve them.

➡ Those who are ready to move on can work on the challenge task which requires children to create a score variable.

Learning Objective
- Use sequence, selection and repeat in programs
- Design and write programs that accomplish specific goals
- Work with variables

Key Vocabulary
- Sequence
- Selection
- Loop
- Variable
- Debug

Resources
- Tissue paper
- Blind-fold
- Wipe off boards & pens
- Scratch program
- Task sheets

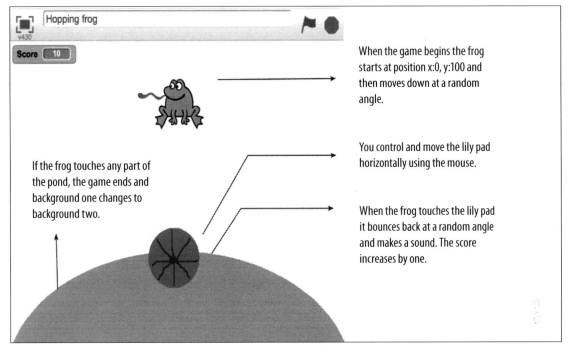

Figure 3.4.1: Hopping frog game

The figure contains the following annotations:

Score 10

When the game begins the frog starts at position x:0, y:100 and then moves down at a random angle.

You control and move the lily pad horizontally using the mouse.

If the frog touches any part of the pond, the game ends and background one changes to background two.

When the frog touches the lily pad it bounces back at a random angle and makes a sound. The score increases by one.

ROUND UP!

Ask the class to share any problems they had when writing their scripts and the strategies that they used to **debug** them. Discuss what else can be done to make this game more interesting and challenging. Select a student who created a score variable as a challenge and ask them to explain their thinking.

ASSESSMENT OPPORTUNITIES

➡ Ask the children to take either a screenshot or a photo of their problems and then discuss the steps they went through to solve them.

➡ Look at the children's completed game designs and task sheets to see if they used repeat loops and variables correctly to complete the task. This can be either a peer or a self-activity and the criteria can be set at the beginning of the session using our My Computing Progress Log found in Chapter 12.

➡ Keep records of their interactions during whole class discussions.

STEP 1: Let's create the backgrounds
- Open Scratch: www.scratch.mit.edu
- Click create tab to start. Right click on the cat sprite and click delete
- Select the stage, and then select the backdrops tab. Click on the paintbrush to draw a pond as below. This is background one
- Duplicate background one and add 'Game over' text at the top

STEP 2: Draw a lily pad sprite
- Click on the paintbrush in new sprite section to paint a new sprite
- Draw a lily pad using circle and line tool. Change the name to 'lily pad'
- Use the centre tool to set the centre as the middle of the circle as shown in this picture

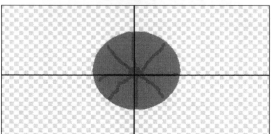

STEP 3: Add the frog sprite
- Click on the choose sprite from library tab in the new sprite section
- Select frog sprite from animals file.
- Your screen should look like this image
- **Please save your game**

STEP 4: Add script to lily pad sprite
We want to move the lily pad horizontally using the mouse
- Set the lily pads coordinates to (x=0, y=−70)
- Add this script to lily pad
- Test your script. What happens?

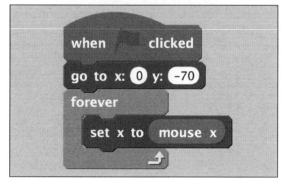

STEP 5: Add script to frog
- We want the frog sprite to start at (x:0, y: 100) coordinates and then move at a random angle between 100 and 220
- Then we create a forever loop and place two if conditionals in the loop
- If the frog touches the lily pad, it bounces back at a random angle between -40 and 40 and play sound 'pop'
- If the frog touches any part of the pond (blue section), it broadcasts game over, waits for one second and then stops the game

STEP 6: Add a script to stage
- We need to write a script to start the game with background one
- When we receive game over broadcast we need to switch to background two
- Save and test your game

```
when [flag] clicked
go to x: 0 y: 100
point in direction pick random 100 to 220
forever
    move 10 steps
    if on edge, bounce
    if < touching lily pad ? > then
        play sound pop
        point in direction pick random -40 to 40

    if < touching color ? > then
        broadcast Game Over
        wait 1 secs
        stop all
```

CHALLENGE!
At the moment there is no score received for successfully controlling the lily pad to stop the frog from touching the pond. Can you create a score variable so that every time frog sprite touches the lily pad score increases by one.

Explain your solution below:

```
when [flag] clicked
switch backdrop to backdrop1

when I receive Game Over
switch backdrop to backdrop2
```

TIME TO CHECK AND DISCUSS
- Can you move the lily pad horizontally using the mouse? What would happen if we use mouse y instead of mouse x?
- When you click on the green flag do frog sprite moves randomly? What happens if you change the value of angles?
- Do frog sprite bounces back at a random angle when it touches to lily pad? Why did we use angle with negative value?

Chapter 4

Computer science unplugged!

By Alessandro Bogliolo

About this chapter

In this chapter children will be introduced to CodyRoby, a do-it-yourself board game based on the key coding principles. The first activity is the construction of the CodyRoby starter game. The subsequent activities provide detailed guidelines to conduct unplugged coding activities by playing with CodyRoby. Each activity is presented as a board game, with its own rules and goals. All the games can be played either on the chessboard included in the kit, or on the floor, possibly using a big chessboard built of soft carpet tiles. Activities are presented in order of increasing complexity, but all of them can be adapted by teachers to address the needs of children in Key Stage 1 – Key Stage 3.

KEY TERMS

Chessboard: CodyRoby board games are conceived to be played either on a chessboard, or on squared paper, or even on the floor.

Cody Cards: playing cards that represent spatial instructions as the blocks of visual programming tools. These are symbols, with no words.

CodyRoby: a method for organizing playful unplugged activities which retain the immediacy and effectiveness of the hour of code

DIY: do-it-yourself.

Move forward: move a step ahead. Represented by a straight arrow on a Cody Card.

Roby: a robot who takes and executes, in sequence, the instructions represented on the Cody Cards, to move on the chessboard.

Turn left: turn to your left without moving. Represented by an arrow pointing to the left on a Cody Card.

Turn right: turn to your right without moving. Represented by an arrow pointing to the right on a Cody Card.

Unplugged activity: activity that does not make use of any electronic device.

ACTIVITIES

1. The construction of the CodyRoby game
2. The race
3. The tourist
4. The duel

CROSS-CURRICULAR

- PE
- Mathematics
- Speaking and Listening

USEFUL LINKS

www.codeweek.it/cody-roby-en/

www.slideshare.net/alessandrobogliolo/inted2015-codyroby

www.ictinpractice.com/codyrobyturning-hour-code-diy-unplugged-game/

http://youtu.be/D5hQ9UTDQ6s

4.1 CodyRoby Game

INTRODUCTION

This activity will enhance the children's engagement by involving them in the construction of the game and allowing them to build their own personalized version of the game. While guiding children in the construction of the game, teachers can point out that they are following instructions step by step, *ie* they are, to some extent, executing a program.

TEACHING SEQUENCE

➡ Watch the video-tutorial available at http://youtu.be/D5hQ9UTDQ6s

➡ Print out all of the sheets in the CodyRoby starter kit. The pdf files are available to download from the official website www. codeweek.it/cody-roby-en/diy-starter-kit/ It is essential to printout all of the pdf files without changing their original size to adapt to the printer. Hence, make sure that 100% is selected as a size option. As for paper thickness, the suggested gramages (grams per square meter) are: 300g for the four sheets of cards, 250g for the box, 150g or lower for the board.

➡ Cut out all the elements of the kit

➡ Decorate the box to add personalization

➡ Fold the box and use the glue stick to keep it in position

➡ Fit all of the elements of the kit into the box. Please pay attention to the video tutorial to see the way in which the chessboard has to be folded in order to fit it into the box.

ROUND UP!

➡ If each child or group of children worked in parallel, invite each child/group to show and motivate the decorations made on the box.

Learning Objective
- Download and print out pdf files
- Cut, fold, and decorate paper
- Become fully aware of the making of CodyRoby

Key Vocabulary
- Sequence
- Algorithm
- Selection
- Loop
- Debug

Resources
- Computer
- Printer
- Paper
- Internet connection
- Scissors, glue stick

➡ With the Cody Cards in hand, teachers can ask pupils to explain which actions they represent. Adopting a trial-and-error approach to find out the exact meaning of the three arrows induce a deeper understanding of the instructions that will be used in subsequent activities. For each card, pupils can be asked either to move on the floor according to the card, or to move a Roby pawn on the board.

ROUND UP!
Did each group:
1. Complete all the steps?
2. Involved all the members?

4.2 The race

INTRODUCTION

The race is a board game for two players (or groups) who draw a random **path** across the chessboard by marking with a pencil all the squares along the path (alternatively grey blocks can be placed along the path). The suggested path length is of eight squares, that can be marked by the two players in turn (*eg* two squares at the time). Cells must be contiguous, *ie* any new cell must share an edge with the previous one.

The pawns are placed at the beginning of the path, while all the Cody Cards available are placed at the sides of the chessboard face up, in order to be easily found and picked up. The cards should be separated by type and stacked into homogenous decks. An object, or a piece of paper, is left on the table close to the chessboard to represent the so-called 'Go' button, which is the button to be touched by the players to start moving their pawns.

Each player has to take the cards from the side decks and place them in **sequence** in front of themselves as fast as possible, composing the sequence of cards to be used to drive Roby (*ie* the pawn) along the path. The player who finishes first presses the go button and tests their solution. This is done by moving the Roby piece along the path according to the instructions provided by the cards. The other player follows the test and tries to find an error. If the solution is correct the fastest player wins.

In spite of the simplicity of the game, it can be very challenging for players of any age and coding experience due to the rush. Moreover, the actual complexity can be tuned by changing the length of the path.

Learning Objective
- Understand that computers need precise instructions
- Design solutions to complete specific tasks

Key Vocabulary
- Path
- Sequence
- Step
- Instruction
- Race

Resources
- CodyRoby game
- Pencil
- Rubber

TEACHING SEQUENCE
STEP 1
➡ Explain the game and possibly watch the video-tutorial available at http://youtu.be/D5hQ9UTDQ6s.

STEP 2
➡ Select two children (or two teams) to play the game.

STEP 3

➡ Unfold the chessboard on the desk and place the players either side of the desk.

STEP 4

➡ Place all the Cody Cards on the desk, face up, possibly divided into three homogeneous decks (Move forward, turn left, turn right).

STEP 5

➡ Either draw the path on the board, or let the two teams compose a random path by adding two squares at the time, in turns.

STEP 6

➡ Start the race and invite the two teams to pick from the decks of cards they need and to put them in sequence (left to right) as fast as possible.

STEP 7

➡ Look out for the team who presses the play button first.

STEP 8

➡ Help the two teams check if the solution provided by the fastest team is correct.

STEP 9

➡ Repeat all the steps from 2 – 8 until all of the children have played at least once.

ROUND UP!

- A sufficient number of cards means teachers can involve the entire class in a race by sketching the chessboard on the blackboard and by asking all the pupils to compose the sequence of instructions required to follow the path.
- Teachers can organize tournaments to engage their pupils in the game.

ASSESSMENT OPPORTUNITIES
Discuss each groups work. Did each group;

1. Win at least once?
2. Involve all team members?
3. Understand the solutions provided by other groups?

4.3 The tourist

INTRODUCTION

The robot game is a traditional informal activity that parents and educators use to develop spatial awareness in pupils. Children pretend to be robots who move in a play area according to the instructions they receive. This is the key mechanism of the spatial-motor activities based on CodyRoby.

In principle, all the CodyRoby board games have their spatial-motor counterpart to be played on the floor. In this case, each square of the chessboard has to be big enough to allow a boy or a girl to stand on it. The ideal material that could be used to build the chessboard are puzzle play mats, but simple sheets of paper placed on the floor can be used as well. Some of the board games require the chessboard to be built entirely, while others require just the squares along a path.

The Tourist is a spatial-motor game to be played by two teams. The gameplay is similar to The Race, with three main differences: i) it entails spatial-motor activity, ii) Roby pieces are replaced by a girl or boy playing the role of the tourist (an impartial referee possibly not belonging to the two teams), and iii) the path leads to the image (ie, either a picture or a drawing) of a monument.

As in The Race, the two teams start by composing a random path. This is done in turn by placing puzzle tiles (or sheets of paper) on the floor. Then a drawing representing a local monument (possibly drawn by the pupils) is placed at the end of the path, while the tourist takes place at the beginning. Cody Cards are divided by type into three decks placed on a school desk. The two teams work on two desks placed at the same distance from the main desk.

The game starts when the tourist asks directions to the monument. The two teams have to run to get the cards they need (one at the time) and

put them in sequence to compose the directions. Then the cards are stacked up in a deck with the first instruction on the top. The team who finishes first provides the instruction stack to the tourist who tests the solution following the instructions under the supervision of the other team. The fastest team wins if the solution is correct.

TEACHING SEQUENCE
STEP 1

➡ Explain the game and engage pupils in drawing one or more monuments of their town.

STEP 2

➡ Select a girl or boy to play the role of the tourist (who walks along the path).

STEP 3

➡ Split the rest of the class into two teams.

STEP 4

➡ Create a path on the floor (start with a very short path of less than five tiles and then increase the length and complexity at subsequent rounds).

STEP 5

➡ Place a monument at the end of the path and the tourist on the first tile.

STEP 6

➡ Tell the tourist to ask for directions to the monument.

STEP 7

➡ Check that the two teams take one card at the time and compose them properly on their desks.

STEP 8

➡ Once the fastest team has provided the instructions to the tourist, help the tourist executing the instructions and check the accuracy of the solution.

STEP 9

➡ Announce the winner of the round.

STEP 10

➡ Go back to step four and start another round!

ROUND UP!

• With a sufficient number of puzzle play mats (or any other kind of tiles) it is possible to build a complex path tree with bifurcations leading to different monuments. It is up to the tourist to decide which monument to ask directions to

• Engage the entire classroom in the design of a third path leading to the main monuments of the town

• Try to bring the game to the real world, asking pupils to find the sequence of instructions really leading from the school to a famous monument

ASSESSMENT OPPORTUNITIES

Discuss each group's work. Did each group:

1. Win at least once?
2. Involve all team members?
3. Understand the solutions provided by other groups?

4.4 The duel

INTRODUCTION

The Duel is a CodyRoby card game for two players or teams. The two players (or teams) use the Cody Cards to move their robots on a 5×5 chessboard in the attempt of catching each other. The game can be played either by moving pawns on the chessboard or by moving real players on a big chessboard built on the floor. For the sake of explanation we refer to the case of a board game with teams represented by pawns.

The two teams place their pawns on two squares at opposite corners of the board. In addition, each team can be allowed to place a block on the board in order to make a square impassable (it is up to the teacher to decide whether the blocks have to be used or not, and how to represent them). The 40 Cody Cards are shuffled and packed in a deck and placed on the desk face down.
Now the duel can start.

At each turn a team takes five cards from the top of the deck keeping them hidden from the other team. If the team has remaining cards in their hand from the last turn, then they take only enough cards from the deck to make their hand of cards amount to five. The team evaluates the five cards in hand and use one or more of them to move its Roby pawn on the board. Moves are made by revealing and dropping one card at a time. The team can decide how many cards to drop in each turn, but it has to drop at least one. The winner is the team which moves its Roby pawn into a square already occupied by the other team's pawn.

There are two exceptions to be regulated:
- if the card deck finishes before the end of the duel, than all the dropped cards are shuffled and used to form a new deck;

Learning Objective
- Debug errors in programs
- Use logical reasoning to predict the behaviour of simple programs

Key Vocabulary
- Duel
- Strategy
- Card game
- Uncertainty

Resources
- CodyRoby game

- if a team makes a wrong move, bringing its piece either out of the board or onto a forbidden square (one of the two occupied by the blocks), then it looses the duel.

TEACHING SEQUENCE
STEP 1
➡ Explain the game and possibly watch the video-tutorial available at http://youtu.be/D5hQ9UTDQ6s.

STEP 2
➡ Select two children (or two teams) to play the game.

STEP 3

➡ Unfold the chessboard on the desk and put players face each other from the two sides of the desk (possibly place two blocks into two squares, in order to make them unpassable).

STEP 4

➡ Shuffle the Cody Cards, place them in a deck, give each team five Cody Cards taken from the top of the deck, face down, and place the rest of the deck on the desk, face down.

STEP 5

➡ Invite the first team to move, *ie* drop the cards (at least one) one at the time and move the pawn accordingly (if this is not the first turn, before moving the team has to take enough cards from the deck to amount their hand of cards to five).

STEP 6

➡ Invite the second team to move (if this is not the first turn, before moving the team has to take enough cards from the deck to amount their hand of cards to five).

STEP 7

➡ Make sure that the two teams keep playing according to steps 5 and 6 until one of the teams catches the other one (if the deck runs out of cards before the end of the duel, then all the cards that have been dropped up to that point need to be shuffled, packed in a deck, and reused). During the game, make sure that no pawns are moved out of the chessboard or into a blocked square. If a team makes a wrong move (*ie* a move that leads the pawn out of the chessboard or into a blocked square) then the other team wins. The same happens if a team is blocked, in that it cannot make a valid move with the cards in hands.

STEP 8

➡ Announce the winner as soon as a team catches the other team's pawn.

STEP 9

➡ Restart from Step 2 until all the pupils have played at least one match.

ROUND UP!

Teachers can organize tournaments to engage the entire class in the game. The tournament can be organized with simultaneous matches if there are a sufficient number of CodyRoby kits.

ASSESSMENT OPPORTUNITIES

Discuss each groups work. Did each group:

- Win at least once?
- Involve all the members?
- Make the right moves?
- Adopt a smart strategy?

Chapter 5

Tinkering time: Adventures in 3D designs

Assoc. Prof. Dr. Selçuk Özdemir & Ahmet Çelik

About this chapter

In this chapter, students will use a free and easy 3D design application, known as Tinkercad. This 3D application is available for everyone to use on tinkercad.com. It does not require any installation. Tinkercad allows users to imagine anything and then design it in minutes using various geometric shapes, numbers, letters *etc*. Designs are saved instantly on the cloud system, so a user can reach their designs from any computer. Tinkercad allows you to create 3D designs that can be printed out from a 3D printer.

KEY TERMS

- Geometric shapes (Tube, Box, Roof, Pyramid, Wedge, Paraboloid, Cylinder, Half Sphere)
- Hole
- Grouping
- Aligning
- Depth

ACTIVITIES

1. Make yourself a keyholder: an anchor
2. Make a cute fish

CROSS-CURRICULAR

All activities can be linked to science, geometry and maths lessons.

LEARNING OBJECTIVES

Use different applications to create and manipulate digital content

TINKERCAD INSTRUCTIONS

Tinkercad runs in any web browser that supports HTML5/WebGL on Windows, Mac or Linux. So, it does not require any installation on a computer and it is easy for young children to use.

3D designs on a Tinkercad workplane can be viewed easily using a mouse with three buttons:

- To navigate around the 3D design, click on the right button of the mouse and move it
- To zoom in or zoom out, scroll the middle wheel of the mouse
- To scroll the workplane to any side of the screen, while pressing SHIFT key on your keyboard click and move the right button of your mouse

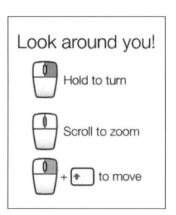

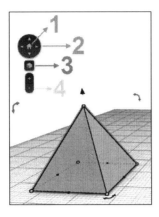

In addition, you can use the functions on the widget that is positioned on the left:

1. Reset view location
2. Rotate view up/right/down/left
3. Fit view to selection
4. Zoom in/out

Shapes are the basic building blocks of Tinkercad. You can use prescribed shape groups involved by geometric, letters, numbers, symbols and extra sections which are located on the right of the screen. You can group together a set of simple shapes or create extremely detailed models.

EDITING SHORTCUTS

While working on geometric shapes, using several shortcuts may help you save time and design easier.

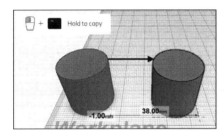

1. For example, when you need a copy of a shape, just press the ALT key on your keyboard and drag it clicking the left button of the mouse to any direction. At the same time, if you press the SHIFT key, you will be able to keep alignment of the copied shape with others.

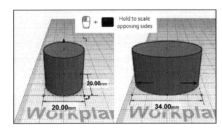

2. While designing a shape's base or height, press the ALT key on your keyboard and drag the side-pointers. As a result, the geometric shape's base and height will be resized proportionally.

3. For a more sensitive rotation on shapes, be careful that the cursor of the mouse is out of the angle circle.

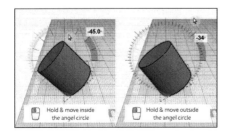

ROUND UP!

Ask the class to share the problems they faced whilst designing the objects on screen and how they solved them. Discuss what else can be done to make these objects more interesting and challenging.

ASSESSMENT OPPORTUNITIES

- Look at the children's completed 3D designs to see if they used all the required shapes, colors, holes and sizes correctly to complete the task.
- Keep records of their interactions during whole class discussions.

USEFUL LINKS

www.tinkercad.com

www.thingiverse.com

http://bilisimgarajakademisi.com

5.1 Make yourself a keyholder: An anchor

INTRODUCTION

In this activity, the students will design their first 3D objects such as an anchor, a fishing boat and a fish. They will learn to use geometric shapes to create new shapes and to resize the shapes. By the end of the activities, students will realize that objects they see on a daily basis are made up of various geometric shapes. The students will merge different geometric shapes to create a new shape while designing an anchor, a fishing boat and a fish. Throughout the activity, they will learn about 3D dimensions.

TEACHING SEQUENCE

➡ Before starting the 3D design activities, make a search on YouTube using the keywords '3D design and 3D printer'. Then, show your students some fascinating scenes of different videos on 3D. Ask the children if they have ever thought about how 3D cartoons are developed. Or whether they have considered how characters in 3D cartoons are designed to look realistic.

➡ Tell the students that they will create their own 3D designs. If you have a 3D printer, you may say that after creating 3D designs on screen, they will be able to print out what they have designed on screen.

➡ Show the children the images opposite and tell them that they will learn how to design these objects.

➡ While designing, tell the children the name of each geometric shape they use and show a real object from your environment containing that geometric shape.

➡ Before the class starts, create user accounts on tinkercad.com. Create a unique user account for each computer in the classroom so that the students can work independently.

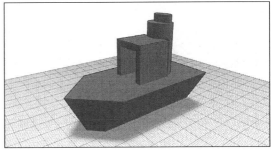

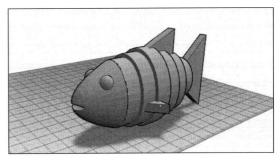

DESIGN STEPS

STEP 1: Create a new design

➡ Create a new Tinkercad design.

➡ Check the image of a real anchor out here. The image below lists the parts of an anchor numbered respectively. In the following steps, each one will be referred to as these numbers. To make it easier, the parts are linked with geometric shapes which will be used in designing that part in Tinkercad.

STEP 2: Add a tube and a box hole

➡ To design part 1, hold the shape of 'tube thin' and drop it somewhere on the workplane.

➡ Select the tube with left button of your mouse. You will see side-pointers positioned in the middle of every side of the shape. The side-pointers are like a black cube. Click on a side pointer and move the cursor to scale up one of its sides to approximately 5-10 mm while holding down the left button. (x=27 mm, y=32 mm, z=3 mm)

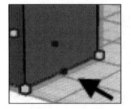

➡ Click on the 'box hole' shape from the tab section named 'holes'. Then, drop a new box hole over the first part, tube. The tube and the hole must be both positioned and aligned as shown in this picture: (x=35 mm, y=20 mm, z>=3 mm)

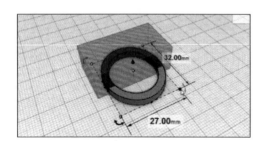

All designs

Here are the designs you have created or which have been shared with you.

Create new design

STEP 3: Make tube and hole one-pieced

➡ We need just half of the tube. To divide the tube into two pieces, use 'box hole', this will help you erase half of the tube.

➡ After, left-click anywhere on the workplane, then start the selection. To select both shapes, hold down the left-button, and move your cursor until both of the shapes are in the selected area. When you are sure that both objects are selected then you can release the left-button.

'Group'
Icon

➡ While both shapes are selected, click on the 'group' icon at the top of page. As soon as you click on group, the parts of the tube included by box hole are grouped, so the parts of the tube are hidden by box hole. If you click on the 'ungroup' icon, you will see the previous shapes again.

STEP 4: Add a box

➡ To design Part 2, add a 'box' shape to the workplane.

➡ Resize the box shape. The sizes should be defined as; x= 5mm, y=25 mm z=3 mm.

➡ Place the box (part 2), in the middle of the tube (part 1). Both shapes should be positioned as shown here.

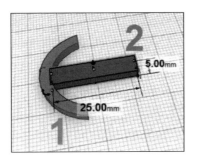

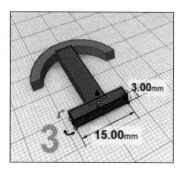

STEP 5: Add an another box with different dimensions

➡ Add a new 'box' shape to the workplane. This is Part 3 of the anchor.

➡ Resize the new box shape. The sizes should be defined as; x=15 mm, y= 3mm, z= 3mm.

➡ Place the new box (part 3) to the edge of the previous one as shown in the image.

STEP 6: Add a roof to complete part 4

➡ Add a 'roof' shape (part 4) to the workplane. Then, rotate the roof vertically as shown in the image. The rotation angle should be 90 degrees .

➡ Lift the roof up 5mm holding the mini black cone. Thus, the roof base sits on the workplane exactly.

➡ Resize the roof. Click on a side-pointer on the roof and move the cursor to scale it up to 10mm x 5mm while holding down the left button. Now, the roof must be smaller.

➡ Drag the roof to the bottom of the divided tube as shown in the picture. Rotate the roof as its sharp edge looks at outside and base edge looks at the tube.

➡ All the parts' height should be the same. So, resize the height of the roof as 3mm.

➡ Place the roof (part 4) as it is merged into the tube. The sharp edge of the roof should be kept out of the tube.

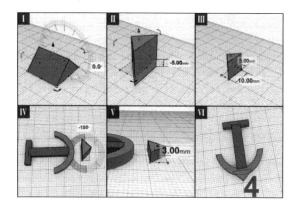

STEP 7: Duplicate roof twice

➡ Now, you will add the same roof shape to both sides of the tube (part 5).

➡ Click on the roof. Then, click the edit menu and duplicate the line at the top of the page.

➡ 'Duplicate' creates a new copy of the roof shape. Drag the new copy of the roof and place it against one of the edges of the tube.

➡ Repeat this process and place another copy of the roof against the other edge of the tube.

➡ You have to rotate both roofs (part 5) added soon so that they are positioned similar to the roofs on the picture below.

STEP 8: Add the keyholder

➡ The design needs a new part so that it can be used as a keyholder once it has been printed out.

➡ Add a new tube thin (part 6) to the workplane.

➡ Resize the tube. The tube base size should be 8 mm. (x=8 mm, y=8 mm, z=3 mm)

STEP 9: Finish your work

➡ The only functional part of this design is the last tube, because if you use it as a keyholder, the last tube will be a connection point.

➡ Part 6 (tube) should be merged with part 3 as shown in the picture below. Drag and drop the tube (part 6) to the edge of part 3. Be careful that part 6 and part 3 should be connected to each other.

➡ All of the parts should be grouped before printing out. After, left-click anywhere on the

workplane, you can start the selection. To select all shapes, hold down the left-button, move your cursor until all of the shapes are in the selected area. When you are sure that all of the parts are selected then you can release the left-button.

➡ Click on the group icon at the top of the page. What you see on the screen should look like the image to the left.

MAKE IT READY FOR 3D PRINTING

➡ To print out your design from a 3D printer, first click the design menu, then select 'Download for 3D printing'.

➡ A warning window will then appear on the screen. Here, click the option '.STL'. As soon as you click, Tinkercad downloads your design as a file with the extension of '.STL'. This is the 3D file type that most 3D printer brands recognise.

➡ Once downloaded, you can open the 3D file on your 3D printer's software.

CHALLENGE

The anchor we designed together has just two arms. Can you design an anchor with four legs for a big ship? Think about what you need to do in order to complete this challenge.

TIME TO CHECK AND DISCUSS

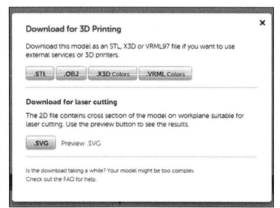

- If you used a 'round roof' for part 1 of this design, what kind of a shape would it be in your opinion?
- The parts of the anchor have sharp edges. To make these sharp edges more rounded and soft, which geometric shapes would you use?
- For part 6 we may need a different shape. Which geometric shapes would you use for part 6 and where would you place it on the anchor?

5.2 Make a cute fish

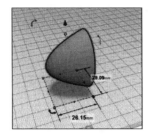

DESIGN STEPS

STEP 1: The head of the fish

➡ Let's start the design from the head of the fish. Add a 'Paraboloid' shape to the workplane.

➡ Then, rotate the paraboloid 90 degrees, as shown in the image to the left.

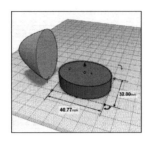

STEP 2: Split the body into cylindrical slices

➡ To design the body of the fish, you may use multiple cylinders, and place them parallel to one another, right up until the fishtail.

➡ Add a 'cylinder' shape to the workplane.

➡ Resize the cylinder's height to 10 mm. It must be lower than its previous height. (x=32 mm, y=40 mm, z=10 mm)

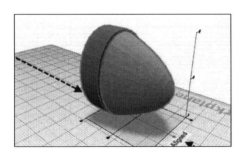

STEP 3: Place the first cylinder along with the paraboloid

➡ Rotate the cylinder 90 degrees. After rotating, place the cylinder so that it touches the paraboloid's cylindrical base.

➡ Then, select both shapes and click the adjust menu and align. Use the center to align both shapes.

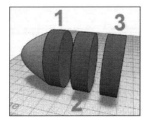

STEP 4: Duplicate the cylinder twice

➡ While pressing the ALT key on your keyboard, click on the cylinder and drag it to the right. You will see a new cylinder. If you press both the ALT and SHIFT keys on the keyboard while dragging the cylinder, the new cylinder will align with the previous one.

➡ Repeat the previous step. You should have three cylinders on the screen.

STEP 5: Create a fish body

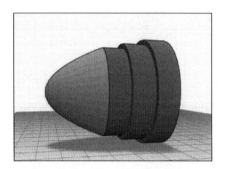

➡ Place all of the cylinders next to each other. Each one should touch another. If you press the SHIFT key on the keyboard while dragging, you will keep the alignment of the slices.

➡ The body of a fish is wider and longer than its head. To simulate a real fish, extend the cylinders' sizes. If needed, lift up the paraboloid and cylinders. Each cylinder to the fish's tail should grow increasingly more.

STEP 6: Complete the body by adding three more cylinders

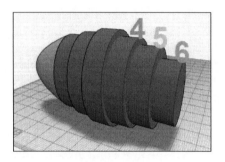

➡ Add three more cylinders to extend the size of the fish.

➡ The width of all cylinders should be 10 to 12 mm.

STEP 7: Add a roof to make the tail

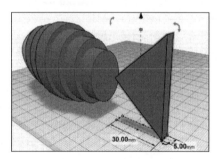

➡ To design the fishtail, add a roof geometric shape to the workplane.

➡ Rotate the roof shape as you see on the picture below. Dimensions: x=5 mm, y=30 mm, z=50 mm.

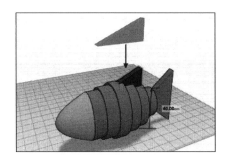

STEP 8: Use a roof to make a dorsal fin

➡ Place the tail next to the body so that both parts touch each other tightly.

➡ Add a new roof shape to the workplane. This will be the dorsal fin. Dimensions: x=5 mm, y=39 mm, z= 17mm

➡ Place the new roof shape on the top of the fish body as shown in the images.

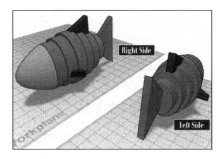

STEP 9: Design the pelvic fins on both sides

➡ Duplicate the dorsal fin twice.

➡ Now, use both of these new shapes to form the pelvic fins on the fish. Place the shapes to the right and left sides of the fish. Rotate them as shown in the image. Usually, pelvic fins are smaller than a dorsal fin.

Dimensions of one of the rotated dorsal fins: x=12 mm, y= 11mm, z= 5mm

STEP 10: Add the eyes and mouth

➡ To design the eyes of the fish, add two 'half sphere' shapes to the workplane. Place each one on the head of the fish, as shown in the image. Dimensions: x=8 mm, y=8 mm, z=5 mm

➡ Finally, you can form the mouth of the fish using a hole. Add a cylinder shape to the workplane. Rotate the cylinder 90 degrees. Click on the cylinder and then click on the hole icon on the inspector frame. Rotated dimensions of the cylinder hole: x=20 mm, y=14 mm, z=4 mm.

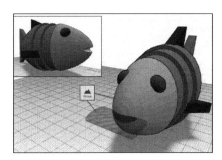

➡ Place the cylinder on the head of fish, so that it creates a mouth. Then, group the paraboloid shape (head of the fish) and the cylinder hole. The mouth of the fish should look similar to the one in the image.

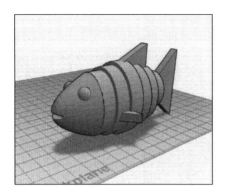

MAKE IT READY FOR 3D PRINTING

➡ To print out your design from a 3D printer, first click the design menu, then select 'Download for 3D printing'.

➡ A warning window will then appear on the screen. Here, click the option '.STL'. As soon as you click, Tinkercad downloads your design as a file with the extension of '.STL'. This is the 3D file type that most 3D printer brands recognise.

➡ Once downloaded, you can open the 3D file on your 3D printer's software.

CHALLENGE

Can you redesign the fish as a goldfish? Have a think about how you could do this. The fins would be different for a goldfish.

TIME TO CHECK AND DISCUSS

· If you replace the roof shape with a pyramid on the fishtail, what would happen to the design. What kind of changes would the pyramid need?
· There are no gills on the fish design. What geometric shapes would you use to design the gills?
· How can you redesign this model as a submarine? What kind of changes would you make? What are the similarities between a fish and a submarine?

Chapter 6

Film, animation and podcasting: let's get creative!

By Ben Sedman

About this chapter

In this chapter, the children will learn how to create a simple film using Windows Movie Maker, use stop frame animation using iMovie, become familiar with Photostory and produce a podcast. A range of interactive activities have been included, which can be modified to meet the needs of children in both Key Stage 1 and Key Stage 2.

KEY TERMS

Digital data: Computers can only work with digital information. Everything that they process must first be turned into a digital signal in one of two states: on or off.
Podcast: a short audio recording which is shared over the internet.
Stop frame animation: an animation technique to make a physically manipulated object or persona appear to move on its own.
Manipulate: handle or control digital data.
Edit: correcting, condensing or modifying.

ACTIVITIES

1. Ready, steady, film! Create your own advert
2. Photo Story 3
3. Speak, record and listen! Create your own podcast
4. Lego or Plasticine? Stop frame animation

CROSS-CURRICULAR

- Literacy (script writing)
- Speaking and listening and drama activities.
- Design and technology (set design) (adverts for food)
- Art (set design)
- Geography (adverts for holidays – locations around the world or in the UK)

USEFUL LINKS

www.windows.microsoft.com/en-gb/windows-live/movie-maker

www.tes.co.uk/teaching-resource/creating-a-superhero-movie-trailer-movie-maker-6184245

www.tes.co.uk/teaching-resource/creating-an-advert-using-powerpoint-and-movie-maker-6327676

http://microsoft-photo-story.en.softonic.com/

www.jakesonline.org/photostory3.pdf

http://beinspiredbyict.blogspot.com/2011/04/photostories-using-photostory-3.html

www.instructables.com/id/How-to-make-a-Lego-stop-motion-construction-movie

www.youtube.com/watch?v=ukFWYe-ZeTw

www.wikihow.com/Make-a-LEGO-Animation

www.bbc.co.uk/podcasts/genre/childrens

www.funkidslive.com

6.1 Ready, steady, film! Create your own advert

INTRODUCTION

This activity will demonstrate to the children how **digital data** can be **stored**, **manipulated** and **edited** on a computer. The children will be given the opportunity to watch and evaluate a range of commercial adverts. They will then create and produce their own advert which will promote a product of their choice. Each advert will be watched and evaluated by the whole class. The completed advert could be shared with another class, during an assembly or on a class blog.

TEACHING SEQUENCE

Overview:
- preparation – look at examples
- purpose – identify an audience
- planning – storyboards and flowcharts
- making – filming and editing
- final outcome – showing the film
- evaluation – reflecting on what worked

➡ Watch and evaluate a range of popular adverts. Use the examples provided for your own. Compete the advert evaluation sheet. (see resource 6.1a overleaf)

➡ Decide on a product and audience the children will be creating an advert for (this could be linked to a topic work in other subjects, *eg* a historical or religious artefact or a healthy snack created in D&T)

➡ Split the class in to small groups. Give each member of the group a different role, *eg* director, camera operator, script editor and actor.

➡ Storyboard and script ideas. Ask the children to highlight speaking parts and how photographs and video will used in different scenes. The storyboard and script

Learning Objective
- Store, manipulate and edit a video on a computer
- Create an advert

Key Vocabulary
- Digital data
- Store
- Manipulate
- Edit
- Video

Resources
- Computers
- Tablets
- Flip cameras
- Chosen product or artifact

worksheets can be used. (see resource 6.1b and 1c overleaf)

➡ When creating the script discuss with the children the use of appropriate language, for example, persuasive language, possible tag lines and catchy phrases.

➡ Demonstrate the filming process using either Flip Cams, a tablet or another portable filming device. Then ask the children to begin filming. Explain to the children that if they film short snippets, they can then be easily edited.

➡ Once you have demonstrated, ask the children to edit their completed videos using the appropriate software. This could be iMovie on iPads, editing software on a Mac, Vimeo, Animoto or Windows Live Movie Player (see resource 6.1d)

ROUND UP!

1. Ask each group to sell their product and play their video the rest of the class. Think Dragons Den or Junior Apprentice! Evaluate the video content.
2. Upload the completed adverts to your class blog or website and share via Twitter!

ASSESSMENT OPPORTUNITIES

1. Discuss each groups work. Did each group;
2. think and behave imaginatively?
3. create an original advert?
4. produce an outcome of value in relation to the objective?
5. able to edit the video content using the software successfully?

Resource 6.1a
Watch and review adverts

Part A: Watch some of the following adverts (or show your own examples)

Collection using persuasive language
https://www.youtube.com/watch?v=azttKmT0rVc

Smash Potato
www.youtube.com/watch?v=U4MTgjNkfyI

Walkers crisps
www.youtube.com watch?v=i7mmXeRvgLo

Christmas Coca Cola
www.youtube.com/watch?v=RUnjQgEDgb4

Part B: Discuss
How were the products advertised?
Which advert did you prefer? Why?
How were characters used?
What persuasive language was included?
Did any of the adverts include slogans?
What type of audience were the adverts aimed at?
How could you improve one of the adverts?

Resource 6.1b

Example storyboard and script

Scene 1

_____

_____

_____

Scene 2

_____

_____

_____

Scene 3

_____

_____

_____

Scene 4

_____

_____

_____

Resource 6.1c
Script for group members:

Advert title	
Scene being filmed	
Location	
Characters in the scene	

Characters	**Speaking parts** (dialogue) ***You could include actions too!***

Resource 6.1d

How to use Windows Live Movie Maker

Equipment:
- A computer (PC or laptop)
- Film editing software: Microsoft Movie Maker (download for free)

How to use software:
1. Click on Start
2. Click on All programmes
3. Click the Windows Movie Maker icon
4. Click Import video and find your first scene of animation
5. Drag and drop the scene into the video timeline
6. Click on Import video again and drag and drop other scenes onto your timeline
7. Click on Make titles or credits
8. Choose which type of title you would like to use
9. Click on Make titles or credits again and add titles to your scenes
10. Click on Import audio or music and find your music
11. Click on Import
12. Drag and drop the music onto the audio/music timeline
13. Click Play to play your film
14. Click Save
15. Name your project and click Save
16. Click Finish movie. Choose which type of format you would like to save your film. Follow the instructions to save it.

6.2 Photo Story 3

INTRODUCTION

This activity will enable the children to create a narrated photostory using **Photo Story**. Photo Story is free application that allows users to create a visual story (show and tell presentation) from their digital photos. The children will be given the opportunity to **evaluate** existing examples and learn how to **import** photographs and **manipulate**, **edit** and **store** them within the application. The children will also learn how to add narration, and music, and will be encouraged to peer assess each other's completed work.

TEACHING SEQUENCE

Overview:
- preparation – look at examples
- purpose – identify an audience
- planning – plan own Photo Story
- making – create Photo Story
- final outcome – share work
- evaluation – reflecting on what worked

➡ Ask the children if they have heard of Photo Story and explain what it is.

➡ Introduce the Photo Story software that the children will be working on. Discuss the features of Photo Story, for example, importing pictures, adding narration and music (see resource 6.2a)

➡ With the children, look at a range of Photo Story resources. Discuss the content.

➡ Demonstrate how to import pictures or photographs (see resource 6.2b). This could be linked to photographs taken during a school visit. The children could create a Photo Story based on their trip to a museum or art gallery.

Learning Objective
- Develop skills in storytelling by learning to use Photo Story 3
- Learn how to manipulate, edit and store a range of media in Photo Story

Key Vocabulary
- Photo Story 3
- Import
- Edit
- Narration
- Evaluate

Resources
- Photo Story
- Internet
- PCs/Laptops
- Digital images
- Music files
- Microphones

➡ Demonstrate how to reorder images on the Photo Story timeline.

➡ Explore with the children how they can use the simple editing techniques to remove black edges, rotate and change colour effects (make photographs black and white or have a charcoal appearance).

➡ Explain to the children that they must save their stories as they work on them to prevent work being lost.

➡ Demonstrate how to add titles to your pictures. Experiment with the colour, font and size of the lettering.

➡ Show how to add narration to your Photo Story by recording your voice and adding it to the tiles.

➡ Customize the motion on the slides by adding transitions, timings, pans and zooms!

➡ Demonstrate how to add background music to your Photo Story. You could use pre-recorded music by the children or sounds from a school trip *eg* animal noises at a zoo.

➡ Finally remind children how to save their story.

➡ Assist children as they work on their own stories. Refer to the checklist (see resource 6.1a) and help sheet (see resource 6.1.b)

ROUND UP!

Get the children to present their Photo Story project for peer evaluation. Did they include all the features on resource 6.1a?

As a class discuss, what made each story effective? Did each presentation have a clear beginning and end? Did the narration support the story? How would they improve their work if they were to repeat it in future?

Extension task

Create a family tree using Photo Story. This could be a historical family tree, for example, for Henry VIII.

Create a Photo Story describing the family and including photographs.

ASSESSMENT OPPORTUNITIES

Were pupils able to:
1. Think and behave imaginatively?
2. Create an original Photo Story?
3. Produce an outcome of value in relation to the objective?
4. Able to edit Photo Story successfully?

Resource 6.2a

Features of Photo Story 3

You can….

- import pictures
- reorder images on your timeline by clicking and dragging
- use simple photo editing to remove black edges, rotate and change colour effects
- add titles to your pictures (change the colour, font and size)
- add narration by recording your voice
- customize the motion of the slides (add transitions, timings, pans and zooms!)
- add background music

Remember to keep saving your story as you work through it!

Resource 6.2b

Follow this link for a step by step guide
www.jakesonline.org/photostory3.pdf

Download Photo Story 3
http://microsoft-photo-story.en.softonic.com/

6.3 Speak, record and listen! Create your own podcast

INTRODUCTION

This activity will demonstrate to the children that a **podcast** is a short **audio recording** which is shared over the **internet**. They will understand that podcasts can be **downloaded** and listened to when it is convenient for the listener.

TEACHING SEQUENCE

Overview:
- preparation – look at podcast examples
- purpose – identify an audience
- planning – decide on podcast content
- making – record and edit podcast
- final outcome – upload podcast
- evaluation – reflect on what worked

➡ Ask the children to choose some of their favourite stories and record themselves reading them out loud.

➡ On a tablet, use Voice Recorder app (see resource 6.3b) or if using a PC, Audacity and a microphone (see resource 6.3a) Remember, a quiet space will be required!

➡ To develop reading skills, the podcasts could be listened to by a younger audience or EAL children within the school. A child could listen to the podcast while they follow the text on the page.

➡ Encourage the children to share their own written stories or poems created during literacy or in other areas of the curriculum, for example, a historical account of Henry VIII or a song created in music, on a podcast.

➡ Create your own class or school radio show! This could include some of the following items and could be embedded on the school website for family members to download.

Learning Objective
- Record, manipulate, upload and download a podcast

Key Vocabulary
- Podcast
- Audio recording
- Internet
- Download
- Audience

Resources
- Podcast
- Audio recording
- Internet
- Download
- Audience

- Have presenters (write a script)
- School news and reminders *ie* swimming lessons, football matches and school clubs
- Review a book or website of the week
- Read out any children's birthdays
- Include information about any special events *eg* class trips

ROUND UP!
Share your podcast!
On your tablet or PC, plug in some headphones, download the podcast and listen. (Click on Voice Record Pro and listen)

ASSESSMENT OPPORTUNITIES
Were pupils able to:
- Think and behave imaginatively?
- Create an original podcast?

Resource 6.3b
How to use the Voice Recorder Pro app.

- Produce an outcome of value in relation to the objective?
- Edit the podcast content successfully?

Resource 6.3a
How to use Audacity – main features (video)
www.youtube.com/watch?v=WmRY5d0uyJo

Stage 1
Open the Voice Recorder App. A tape player will appear.

Stage 2
Press record. The tape will start to play and a green light will appear.

Stage 3
Save your recording. Give it a name.

Stage 4
Plug in your earphones and listen to your recording. Watch the sound bar move as you listen!

6.4 Lego or Plasticine? Stop frame animation

INTRODUCTION

This activity will demonstrate to the children how **stop frame animation** can be **filmed** and **edited** using iMovie on an iPad. The children will be given the opportunity to watch and evaluate examples of stop frame animations. They will then create their own versions demonstrating how to create movements and transitions within their animations. The edited animation will be evaluated and could be shared on a class blog or website!

TEACHING SEQUENCE

Overview:
- purpose – identify an audience
- planning – storyboards and scripts
- making – filming and editing
- final outcome – showing the animation
- evaluation – reflecting on what worked

- Discuss what stop frame animation is. Explain that it is a technique which is used to make a stationary object appear as if it was moving.
- Show the children a range of stop start animations. Show examples that they may have watched on television and examples made by other children at home or in school. (see resource 6.4a) Discuss what makes a good stop frame animation, for example, using figures (characters), including a set, good lighting and including dialogue and music.
- Arrange the children into small groups. Give each group member a specific role *eg* camera person, script editor, voice over actor.
- Ask each group to create a storyboard (see resource 6.1b) or flowchart (use Lego figures or Plasticine). Link to topic work (*eg* e-safety) or texts covered during literacy. Identify the audience the animations are being made for.

Learning Objective
- Use iMovie to create a stop frame animation
- Manipulate, edit and store a stop frame animation

Key Vocabulary
- Stop frame animation
- Edit
- Film
- Frames
- Movements
- Transitions

Resources
- iPad/iPod Touch
- Video editing software: iMovie

- Create a script for the dialogue. (see resource 6.4c)
- Design the set (Make it out of Lego, card and/or Plasticine).
- Start filming! Take a photograph (frame) using the iPad camera each time an action, set or camera angle changes. Demonstrate this first to the children

TIP – The most realistic movements occur when there is only a little movement between each frame.

ROUND UP!

1. Upload photographs to iMovie (see resource 6.4d)
2. Share stop frame animations
3. Evaluate each other's animations (see resource 6.4e)
4. Share animations on a class blog, website or via Twitter!

Have you tried...

Pivot stick animator http://pivotanimator.net. This free program allows children to create short animations with on-screen stick figures. Children can create all kinds of moving characters and backgrounds for their animations.

ASSESSMENT OPPORTUNITIES

Were pupils able to:

1. Think and behave imaginatively?
2. Create an original stop frame animation?
3. Produce an outcome of value in relation to the objective?
4. Able to edit the video content using iMovie successfully?

Resource 6.4a

Stop frame animation examples:

On television:

Morph
www.youtube.com/watch?v=zvewIE5UoME

Wallace and Gromit
www.youtube.com/watch?v=t8T8bStabq0

Shaun the Sheep
www.youtube.com/watch?v=BQeI4i2Nzw8

Bagpuss
www.youtube.com/watch?v=t9beAp3TG2E

The Adventures of Portland Bill
www.youtube.com/watch?v=wGdkfhYSlPw

Postman Pat
www.youtube.com/watch?v=q1cQDO30qOQ

The Wombles
www.youtube.com/watch?v=XaC3jtlGHJw

Made by children:

www.youtube.com/watch?v=36PrILMIA30

www.radiowilbury.org.uk/

http://goo.gl/8Z70St

Resource 6.4c

Script for stop frame animation

Animation title	
Scene being filmed	
Location	
Characters in the scene	

Characters	Speaking parts (dialogue) You could include actions too!

Resource 6.4d

iMovie for beginners
https://www.youtube.com/watch?v=ZGG5kbMKmLo

iMovie Guide
http://iosguides.net/app-guides/imovie-for-ipad/

Resource 6.4e

Animation evaluation!

Was the storyline clear? Why?

Did the setting work? Why?

How were the movements and transitions?

Did the integration of audio work? Why?

Any improvements you would make?

What was your favourite part and why?

Chapter 7

Embedding computing in science

By Maggie Morrissey

In this chapter the children will learn a variety of ways to use technology to support the teaching and learning of science. Data logging will help support a variety of areas of science such as measuring and recording investigations, especially when measuring sound. Using Skype along with concept cartoons will help children to develop argumentation skills; these skills are a common and essential feature in the science community but are often overlooked in our school system. Digital cameras have huge potential to support children's learning in science, from observation skills through to recording and evaluating children's investigations this ubiquitous and but often underused resource holds great potential to enthuse children when learning science.

KEY TERMS

Data logging: data collection taken automatically using a computer over a specific time.

Sensor: a device that responds to some form of input from the physical environment *eg* sound, light and temperature.

Sensing: the act of recording input from the physical environment using sensors.

Snapshot mode: allows you to capture sensor readings when needed, rather than at regular timed intervals.

Computer mediated communication: communication that occurs between humans through electronic devices, these can be synchronous such as Skype or asynchronous which involves blogs and emails.

Argumentation skills: Using evidence in science to decide if a science idea should be accepted or rejected. The process skills involve discussion and evaluation of the idea.

ACTIVITIES

1. Introduction to data logging
2. Making ear muffs for my teacher
3. Using Skype to develop argumentation skills
4. Using a digital camera in science fieldwork

CROSS-CURRICULAR

- Making ear muffs activity can be linked to Design and Technology. Children can design and then make the ear muffs using the materials that have been shown to be more efficient.
- Skype discussions will of course involve a lot of speaking and listening within literacy. To add another layer, children could be connected with children in other countries. This provides excellent learning opportunities in geography.
- Using a digital camera can also be linked to art projects. Images collected could help to develop a class database as part of the Computing Curriculum. Writing up and using images in an online magazine or other multimedia presentations will develop literacy skills.

USEFUL LINKS
Introduction to data logging
Primary data logging suppliers
www.data-harvest.co.uk/catalogue/science/primary/datalogging

www.logitworld.com/index.php/primary-junior/primary-data-loggers

User guide for EasySense Vu
www.data-harvest.co.uk//docs/uploads/ds121_2_vu_user_guide.pdf

Skype discussions
Where to purchase concept cartoons
www.conceptcartoons.com

The Astra Zeneca site explains concept cartoons in more depth
www.pstt.org.uk/ext/cpd/dips/concept-cartoons.htm

Using a digital camera in science fieldwork
How to use a digital camera
www.wikihow.com/Take-a-Picture-with-a-Digital-Camera

How to upload images to a computer
www.wikihow.com/Transfer-Images-from-a-Digital-Camera-to-a-Computer

How to identify specimens found and contribute to the online database
www.ispotnature.org/communities/global

Digital Camera for Key Stage 1
Vtech have a good range of cameras that look like toys, but are fully functional, their size helps little hands hold onto them easily.
www.vtech.co.uk

7.1 Introduction to data logging

INTRODUCTION

This activity will introduce the children to the basic features of **data logging**, in particular the use of the snapshot mode. It is suitable for upper Key Stage 1 and lower Key Stage 2 classes or in fact any class that has not used data logging equipment and software before. The equipment used here was Data Harvest Easy Sense Vu but this session will work with other equipment such as the Logit Explorer Datalogger.

TEACHING SEQUENCE

➡ Show the children the data logger. Do they know what data logging is? Are there any clues in the words? What does the word sense mean?

➡ Get another adult to write up children's ideas onto a whiteboard. Is this word linked to the others on the display? Sense, sensor, sensing. What class of words are these? Can they make quick sentences using these words? Do this with their talk partners. This particular activity is essential when working with children who do not have English as an additional language. They need to be aware of using these words not just as nouns but verbs also.

➡ Clarify the meaning of sensing so that the whole class is confident with this. Explain that the equipment can sense three types of conditions: sound, light and temperature.

➡ Connect the data logger to the computer and show the main software on the whiteboard.

➡ Start up the Easy-Sense software, then choose the snapshot mode and ask the class to be as quiet as they can. Use snapshot to record the children being quiet.

Learning Objective
- To learn what data logging is
- Use different tools and applications to collect and present information
- To learn how to take a snapshot reading

Key Vocabulary
- Sense
- Sensor
- Sensing
- Data
- Meter
- Measuring

Resources
- Data logger
- Vocabulary sheets 7.1a

➡ Now ask everyone to come close and make a loud noise. This could be clapping or calling out. You might want to choose this depending on how large the classroom is. Press snapshot section and record the data.

➡ Ask the class to move back to the center of the class, repeat the noise making, and recording.

➡ Ask the class to all move to the back of the class and repeat the noise making and recording.

➡ You should have four bars on the screen, a short one (quiet) a very tall one (noise close up) *etc.*

➡ Ask the children what the graphs show. If the children are unsure; explain that big bars are more, small bars are less. See if they can recognise where they were in the class with each reading.

➡ Depending on the age and ability of the children, explain in more detail about each axis.

➡ Tell them that they can use the data logger away from the computer and then repeat the investigation using the logger disconnected from the computer. This time, get some of the children to press snapshot (which is on the unit) whilst recording the sound. Draw their attention to the number of recordings that have been taken.

➡ Reconnect the unit to the computer and using the remote function on the interface to retrieve the second set of recordings. Most recent work appears at the top of the list.

ASSESSMENT OPPORTUNITIES

1. Do children understand how the graph has been made?
2. Can they read the intervals on the graph?
3. Can they identify the quiet/medium and loud sounds?

Continued work
Who is the noisiest in the class?
Who can make the most noise at five metres?
Investigate the noisiest class in the school

Key Vocabulary – 7.1a

data logger	temperature	range
sense	light	display
sensor	meter	snapshot
sensing	measuring	monitoring
sound	data	

7.2 Making ear muffs for my teacher

INTRODUCTION

This activity moves on from the introduction session and gives the children a focus for using the data logging equipment. It should also follow on from class work where children have learnt how sound travels through different materials.

This activity could be covered as a whole class but ideally each group should have their own plan. This will then allow them later to discuss any errors or differences in their results adding the extra science process skill of argumentation.

TEACHING SEQUENCE

➡ Show the children a picture of yourself or another adult trying to block out sound *eg* pillows held to their ears is one example. Explain that there is a problem with noisy neighbours and the teacher is having problems sleeping at night. Can they help? Discuss with the class the problem of noise pollution; have they had noisy neighbours? How did it make them feel? Was their family affected?

➡ Show the children a selection of materials and ask them to decide which one they think is the better material for earmuffs. Ask children to vote on which material and then list them in order of popularity.

➡ Show the children the science-planning sheet. Explain that as a group they are going to plan their investigation and fill in the sheet together. However, they must make their own prediction. This can be different from their partners. Encourage them to give a reason for their prediction.

➡ Introduce them to the recording sheet, explain they will have to note which material is used with each recoding when they use

Learning Objective
- To be able to plan a test to measure how well different materials muffle sound
- To be able to make a prediction
- To make a fair test
- Use different tools and applications to collect and present information

Key Vocabulary
- Decibel dB
- Predict
- Sound sensor
- Materials

Resources
- Data logger, sound sensor and PC
- Range of materials *eg* bubble wrap, wool, synthetic materials
- Empty box
- Buzzer or other sound source
- Investigation planning sheet 7.2a
- Group recording sheet 7.2b

the snapshot – refer back to the previous lesson.

➡ Discuss with them the need for taking more than one measurement for each material. Why do they think it is a good idea?

→ When the groups are ready they can take turns to carry out the investigation. If individual groups are going to undertake the investigation, it is a good idea to do this in a quiet area such as the library. Another adult such as a teaching assistant could supervise the work.

ASSESSMENT OPPORTUNITIES

1. Have all children made their own prediction? Reassure them that this is not about having a right or wrong answer.
2. Has each child given a reason for why they think a material would be better for muffling sound?
3. Have they devised a fair test and recorded their work onto the recording sheet?

LESSON 7.2b GROUP RECORDING SHEET

Materials	Reading 1	Reading 2	Reading 3	Average
1				
2				
3				

(LESSON 7.2a GROUP PLANNING BOARD is overleaf)

LESSON 7.2a GROUP PLANNING BOARD

Group Planning Board

Our question to be answered

_____

My Prediction _____

We will change

We will measure

We will keep these things the same

7.3 Using Skype to develop argumentation skills

INTRODUCTION

Argumentation is an essential part of science learning. Scientists rarely work in isolation, and often collaborate and have their work peer reviewed. This is something that is shown to be lacking in science teaching in general, in both primary and secondary sectors. This activity introduces the idea of using **Computer-Mediated Communication** (CMC) such as Skype to bring children together to discuss their views and ideas about science.

Organisation/differentiation: This activity could be undertaken as a whole class but is more suitable and recommended for small groups. No more than six children, three from each class. Prior to discussions agree with children rules on small group discussions.

EAL children: This is a very useful activity to support children who are learning English. You may need to consider having a vocabulary board covering the topic near to the children to offer support during the discussions.

This level of work is mainly for Key Stage 2 – however a whole class discussion using the concept cartoons as a focus is worth trying in a year two class.

Learning Objective
- To be able to consider alternative views
- To be able to listen and contribute to a discussion
- To make predictions and explain why they believe in this view

Key Vocabulary
- Argumentation
- Prediction
- Hypothesis
- Computer Mediated Communication
- Web conference
- Web cam

Resources
- Concept cartoon or other similar stimulus such as a photograph or key question
- Skype, web cam
- Internet
- Pencils/pens/highlighters

TEACHING SEQUENCE

➡ Teachers on either side of the classroom connect to their partner class using Skype. After preliminary introductions and social talk explain to the children that they are going to discuss common ideas about their science topic.

➡ Teachers give children the chosen concept cartoon and ask them to number each statement using a pencil or highlighter. Allow children time to read quietly and give them some thinking time about the statements in the cartoon.

➡ Get children to take turns to read each statement – this turn taking must involve both classes.

→ Now ask children to decide which statement they most agree with. Encourage them to explain to the group their reasons for this choice.

→ At this stage it is recommended that teachers move away from the groups and allow the children to work independently, only intervening when the children need something clarified.

→ When the children have finally decided on their own theories encourage them to write down why they believe this on their concept cartoon.

→ Now decide which is the most popular idea and get them to consider how they would show this to others in the groups who have a different view. What sort of investigation could they do?

→ Children who have an alternative idea should also plan their investigation.

→ Children could then use the investigation-planning sheet that is in lesson 7.2 to plan their work.

→ At the end of the session get the children to agree to meet via Skype after the investigation has taken place. In this session or other sessions children can discuss the limitations and successes of their work. They could also discuss any changes they made to their practical work and why.

→ The children from each school should then return to their classmates and explain how the session went and what ideas came about. This will then lead on to the whole class participating in their own investigations that may be similar or completely different.

Important point: Do not be surprised that after the discussions some children may change their predictions and even their practical work. Do not be tempted to keep to the plan, this change of idea is a normal development in science and will be a good talking point as the work develops.

ASSESSMENT OPPORTUNITIES

•   Have all of the children participated in the discussion?
•   Have children listened to others views and even suggested alternative ideas?
•   Did each make a prediction? (Some children worry about having the correct answer)

Additional assessment task – optional
It may be worth considering video recording the interaction between the two classes, as this would give teachers and children and chance to look back at how their ideas and plans may have changed

Concept cartoon example

Concept cartoon images can be found easily via internet searches, but ideally a school should try and purchase the book with or without the CD-ROM. The book and CD-ROM explains the science behind the cartoons and common misconceptions that children have. The book can be found here: http://conceptcartoons.com/science.html

7.4 Using a digital camera in science fieldwork

INTRODUCTION

Taking children outside to undertake fieldwork is an exciting and interesting part of science learning. Using a digital camera will help to not just record the children working but also the specimens that they found and the location of these. These images will last longer than the items taken back to class and will provide a long-term image to support class discussions about their work. The images of course can then be used in other multimedia presentations such as PowerPoint, Photo Story 3, and blogs that will provide a more interesting way for children to write up their science work.

Organisation/differentiation: Mixed ability groups of no more than six children in each group. Depending on the location they may or may not need adults with each group. Depending on group dynamics, it may be easier to keep one child as the photographer whilst others are looking for specimens. However, they can agree as a group if they want to share this task.

This resource is suitable for both Key Stage 1 and Key Stage 2.

TEACHING SEQUENCE

➡ Demonstrate the basic features of the camera. Show them how to hold the camera properly to prevent camera shake. How to zoom in, but more importantly explain that to focus their image they need to hold down the photo button slightly before taking the image. More instructions can be found online: www.wikihow.com/Take-a-Picture-with-a-Digital-Camera

➡ Give each child a clipboard with an A4 card attached. Explain that they should use the

Learning Objective
- To be able to use a simple digital camera
- To develop observational skills
- To understand how to collect data outside of the classroom

Key Vocabulary
- Argumentation
- Prediction
- Hypothesis
- Computer Mediated Communication
- Web conference
- Web cam

Resources
- Digital camera
- Focus
- Zoom
- Habitat
- Fungi
- Specimens
- Fieldwork

sticky tape to put the specimens onto the card.

➡ Explain that they can make a note as to where they found the item, or preferably take a picture of its location.

→ Ask children not to remove new shoots from trees or plants but to photograph them instead. Encourage them to discuss in their groups what they see happening around the new shoot.

→ At this stage it is worth explaining that they should not be touching certain plants or fungi (This will depend on the location of the fieldwork) and when they return to class they should wash their hands.

→ Encourage them to respect any small creatures such as spiders, earthworms and woodlice that they may come across. They have an important role in the local habitat. Get them to photograph any insects they see.

→ Children now go out and start their work.

→ When they return to class, A4 cards with samples should be labelled with names or a group number. The camera used should also be recorded so that the images can be linked to the samples.

→ Upload images as soon as possible to a laptop, computer or tablet. Instructions can be found online: www.wikihow.com/Transfer-Images-from-a-Digital-Camera-to-a-Computer

Further work

With the images and specimens the children can then try to identify them. Explain that it is ok to make their own name for their item based on the features that they observe. This is what past scientists/explorers did. They could then go on to use following website: www.ispotnature.org/communities/global from the Open University to identify their items and learn more about what they have found.

ASSESSMENT OPPORTUNITIES

- Have children using the cameras understood how to use focus and zoom?
- Are they observing features of samples found and their location?
- Are they recording images and collecting the samples correctly?

Images from a recent fieldwork trip on school grounds

Chapter 8

Linking mathematics and computing

By Sue Pope

About this chapter

This chapter includes starting points for mathematical exploration using digital technology that will develop children's skills both in mathematics and computing. The Becta entitlement documents (reworked in 2009 by the National Strategies are now available in the STEM e-library) identified six major opportunities for learners to use ICT in learning mathematics: learning from feedback; observing patterns; seeing connections; exploring data; teaching the computer, and developing visual imagery. These opportunities may be developed through a wide range of ICT – standard and graphic calculators, spreadsheets, interactive software on CD or online.

The JMC report on digital technologies (2011) stated:
Einstein famously said that his pencil was more intelligent than he was – meaning, that he could achieve far more using his pencil as an aid to thinking than he could unaided. There is a need to recognise that mathematical digital technologies are the 'pencils of today' and that we will only fully exploit the benefits of digital technologies in teaching, learning and doing mathematics when it becomes unthinkable for a student to solve a complex mathematical problem without ready access to digital technological tools.

The programme of study for computing states:
A computing education also ensures that pupils become digitally literate – able to use, and express themselves through, information and communication technology – at a level suitable for the future workplace and as active participants in a digital world. In the programme of study for computing children in Key Stage 1 are expected to understand what algorithms are and to write and test simple programs and in Key Stage 2. They are expected to use sequence, selection, and repetition in programs and work with variables and various forms of input and output. They are also expected to select, use and combine a variety of software (including internet services) on a range of digital devices to accomplish given goals, including collecting, analysing, evaluating and presenting data and information.

KEY TERMS

Learning from feedback

The computer often provides fast and reliable feedback, which is non-judgemental and impartial. This can encourage children to make their own conjectures and to test out and modify their ideas.

Observing patterns

The speed of computers and calculators enables learners to produce many examples when exploring mathematical problems. This supports their observation of patterns and the making and justifying of generalisations.

Seeing connections

The computer enables formulae, tables of numbers and graphs to be linked readily. Changing one representation and seeing changes in the others helps learners to understand the connections between them. Working through a medium which enables learners to switch effortlessly between these representations enhances their conceptual development.

Exploring data

Computers enable learners to work with real data, which can be represented in a variety of ways. This supports interpretation and analysis.

'Teaching' the computer

When learners design an algorithm (a set of instructions) to make a computer achieve a particular result, they have to express their commands unambiguously and in the correct order. They are beginning to model particular behaviours or develop a set of rules. This engagement with a 'formal system' sets up the opportunity for developing a mathematical habit of mind, to develop their skills of algebraic thinking.

'Teaching the computer' encourages learners to formalise their mathematical thinking, define conditions, sequence actions and express their ideas clearly. When the computer carries out the instructions it has been given, learners need to observe the effect, and if necessary refine and improve the procedure they taught the computer.

Developing visual imagery

Using a computer enables learners to manipulate diagrams dynamically. This not only supports learning by producing actual diagrams and graphs, it also encourages learners to predict the results and to visualise the geometry as they generate their own mental images. The facility to generate many examples also helps learners to notice 'what changes and what remains the same' and enables them to formulate and test their conjectures.

ACTIVITIES

1. Rich aunt
2. Constructing regular polygons in Logo
3. Messing up
4. Which cup is better?
5. Mini enterprise: How much should I charge?

CROSS-CURRICULAR

- Mathematics
- Science
- Financial literacy

USEFUL LINKS

JMC (2011) Digital technologies and mathematics education
www.nationalstemcentre.org.uk/res/documents/page/JMC_Digital_Technologies_Report_2011.pdf

Becta (2009) Primary Mathematics with ICT: A pupil's entitlement to ICT in primary mathematics
www.nationalstemcentre.org.uk/elibrary/resource/4537/primary-mathematics-with-ict-a-pupil-s-entitlement-to-ict-in-primary-mathematics

8.1 Rich aunt

INTRODUCTION

This task invites children to respond to a letter from an elderly relative who offers money. The children need to generate the sequences and sum them in order to make an informed decision. A spreadsheet is an ideal tool as it allows the computations to be completed accurately and the outcomes to be represented graphically.

TEACHING SEQUENCE

Overview:

- preparation – work in groups and read the letter
- purpose – what do they think might be best?
- planning – decide on how to model the situation
- modelling – create a spreadsheet using appropriate formulae
- investigation – explore what happens over different time periods and graph the results
- conclusion – draw conclusions and write a reply to the letter
- evaluation – reflection on the process and compare letters with other groups

➡ Children get into groups to discuss the letter and consider possible responses.

➡ Each group uses a spreadsheet to model the different scenarios – both the amount each year and the total received.

➡ Each group investigates and selects an appropriate graph to represent their results (note a scatterplot is best).

➡ Each group draws conclusions and writes a response.

Learning Objective
- Use a spreadsheet to create a mathematical model to make a decision.
- Use different tools and applications to collect and present information

Key Vocabulary
- Spreadsheet cell
- Spreadsheet formula
- Scatterplot
- Sequence
- Sum

Resources
- Spreadsheet program on laptops or tablets

ROUND UP!

Share letters

Groups look at one another's letters and evaluate their own response.

ASSESSMENT OPPORTUNITIES

Were children able to:

1. Understand the task and create a spreadsheet model?
2. Generate a suitable graph?
3. Justify their chosen option?
4. Critique their conclusions?

Resource 8.1a

Jo has a rich aunt who is a mathematician, she has written the letter below to Jo.
Please prepare a reply.

Sum House
Addington
A1 23B

Dear Jo

Today is my 70th birthday and I would like to give you some money, as I'm not getting any younger!

I would like to give you some money each year starting now, using one of the methods below:

1. £100 this year, £90 the next, £80 the next and so on.
2. £10 this year, £20 the next, £30 the next and so on.
3. £10 this year, 1.5 times the next, 1.5 times the next and so on.
4. £1 this year, £2 the next, £4 the next, £8 the next and so on.

I can only give you money while I am alive!
Please let me know which method you would prefer and why.

I look forward to hearing from you.

Love

Aunt Chris

Resource 8.1b

Use a spreadsheet as a modelling tool

1. How to generate the counting numbers in a column: put the first number in a cell *eg* A2, in cell A3 type =A2+1, then copy this formula down.
2. Any sequence can be generated by adjusting the input number and the instruction in the formula. Note that any formula begins with =
3. Summing a sequence: if the sequence is in column A, starting with A2, and the sum is in B use the formula in B2, =A2 and in B3, =B2+A3. The latter should be copied down.
4. To create a graph, highlight the cells with the data and go to Insert graph. When looking for relationships a scatterplot is the most appropriate representation.

The example below shows what happens if you start with £5 and get an additional £5 each year.

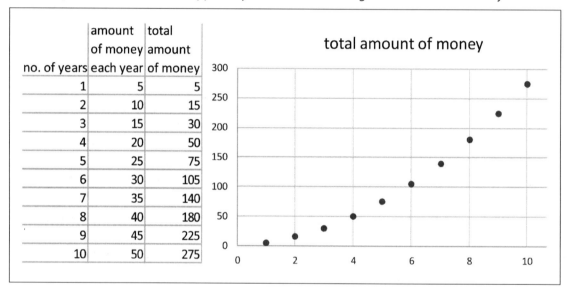

no. of years	amount of money each year	total amount of money
1	5	5
2	10	15
3	15	30
4	20	50
5	25	75
6	30	105
7	35	140
8	40	180
9	45	225
10	50	275

8.2 Constructing regular polygons in Logo

INTRODUCTION

This task builds on children's early experiences of using programmable toys to find their way through mazes and follow particular routes. The MSW Logo is freely available and is relatively intuitive to use.

TEACHING SEQUENCE

Overview:
- preparation – work in pairs and gain familiarity with Logo
- purpose – can you draw a square?
- planning – try out ideas and decide how to draw a square of any size
- programming – introduce the command repeat and how to indicate variables
- investigation – explore how to draw other regular polygons
- extension – what happens if the turning angle does not divide exactly into 360 degrees? Can you fill the screen with identical regular polygons?
- evaluation – presenting work and explaining how it was made

➡ Children get into pairs to experiment with Logo and understand how the commands work: FD Forward, BK Backward, RT Right, LT Left, PU Pen up, PD Pen down

➡ Each pair is challenged to draw a square. Can they draw a square of any size? Can they draw a design made of squares?

➡ Share strategies and introduce the command repeat, and teach the computer a command using a variable eg

TO SQUARE :s
REPEAT 4 [FD :s RT 90]
END

Learning Objective
- To develop simple programmes in Logo to draw regular polygons and related designs.
- Use sequence, selection and repeat in programs

Key Vocabulary
- Logo commands
- Teaching the computer
- Variables
- Testing conjectures

Resources
- Logo program on laptops or tablets Or visit www.j2e.com/logo.html

➡ Can they draw other regular polygons? – encourage children to experiment by walking around various polygons so they realise that they make a full turn however many sides they walk around.

➡ Some may create designs by covering the screen with identical regular polygons with no gaps (regular tessellations), others may investigate overlapping polygons, or what happens if the turning angle does not divide exactly into 360 degrees.

ROUND UP!

Pairs share their work and explain how it was generated. A classroom display could be created.

ASSESSMENT OPPORTUNITIES

Were children able to:

1. Write a programme to create a regular polygon?
2. Generate their own design?
3. Systematically explore a development idea?
4. Explain how they generated their design/pattern?

Resource 8.2

Constructing regular Polygons

Look at the code below and guess the shape that it will create. REPEAT 3 [FD 100 RT 120]	**The shape is:**
Write the script to draw an Octagon 	**The script is:**
To generate a square of any side length (:s) TO SQUARE :s REPEAT 4 [FD :s RT 90] END	**To generate a regular polygon with (:n) sides** TO POLYGON :s :n REPEAT :n [FD :s RT 360/:n] END
Using pen up (PU) and (PD) commands children can generate a wide variety of designs. **Note that it is possible to use recursion in Logo.**	

8.3 Messing up!

INTRODUCTION

This task invites children to create a drawing in a **dynamic geometry package** such as Geogebra, which is free. Dynamic geometry allows children to create drawings using various geometric tools. These drawings can be manipulated using the hand tool. Only if children use the geometric properties of their drawing to relate the various components will the drawing be robust when it is manipulated.

TEACHING SEQUENCE

Overview:

- introduction – show a square made of connected line segments – what is this? Use the hand tool to show how it does not stay a square for long!
- preparation – work in pairs and gain familiarity with the dynamic geometry package, construct a robust square
- purpose – can you draw a house which will always look like a house?
- exploring – try out ideas and decide how to draw a house that can't be 'messed up'
- investigation – what sort of constructions keep objects related?
- extension – create a complex design that can't be messed up
- evaluation – present work and explain how it was made

➡ Illustrate 'messing up' with a simple design *eg* a square made of unconnected line segments. Children get into pairs to experiment with the dynamic geometry package and understand how the tools work. Can they produce a robust square?

➡ Each pair is challenged to draw a house. Can they draw a house which maintains the

Learning Objective
- To construct drawings whose components are related so they can not be 'messed up'

Key Vocabulary
- Dynamic geometry tools
- Perpendicular, parallel, intersection
- Testing conjectures

Resources
- Dynamic geometry on laptops or tablets

relationships between objects, so it doesn't get 'messed up' when dragged about?

➡ Draw other designs, patterns and objects that cannot be 'messed up'

ROUND UP!

Pairs share their work and explain how it was generated. A classroom display could be created.

ASSESSMENT OPPORTUNITIES

Were children able to:

1. Create a robust square?
2. Generate their own robust drawing?
3. Explain how they generated their drawing?

Resource 8.3

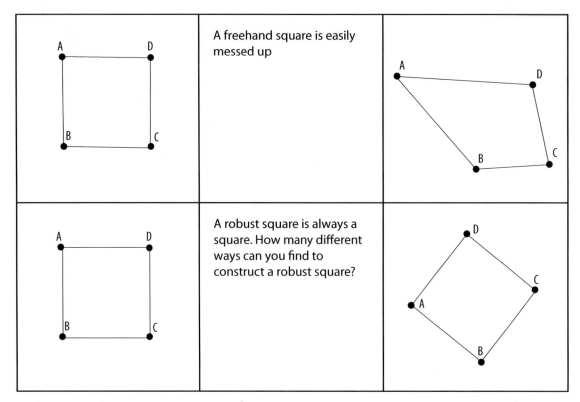

[square ABDC]	A freehand square is easily messed up	[distorted quadrilateral ABDC]
[square ABDC]	A robust square is always a square. How many different ways can you find to construct a robust square?	[tilted square ABDC]

You could use the regular polygon tool, or the geometric tools to construct parallel and perpendicular lines and the circle tool to transfer lengths.

8.4 Which cup is better?

INTRODUCTION
This task invites children to use technology to record and analyse data collected during a practical science/technology experiment.

TEACHING SEQUENCE
Overview:
- introduction – which of these disposable cups is best for a warm drink?
- preparation – work in groups and plan how they might conduct a 'fair' test – likely to include how well the cup retains warmth but may also have to do with other properties of the materials
- purpose – which cup is better?
- exploring – what sort of experiments could be conducted? Does the capacity of the cup matter? Does the nature of the drink matter *eg* soup or tea?
- investigation – conduct experiments that result in data (*eg* temperature of drink against time)
- conclusion – draw conclusions giving reasons for the decisions made
- evaluation – present work and compare conclusions with other groups

➡ Begin with showing a variety of disposable cups. Which is better? How can you decide? Ensure the notion of a 'fair' test is introduced.

➡ In small groups design a 'fair' test, or series of tests to help them make the decision.

➡ Conduct the experiments. Record the data in a spreadsheet and generate a scatterplot of the data.

Learning Objective
- To use technology to record and analyse data and draw conclusions

Key Vocabulary
- Insulator
- Strength
- Temperature
- Criteria for selecting the better cup
- Experimental design

Resources
- Variety of disposable cups – plastic polystyrene, paper, card
- Thermometers, stop watches
- spreadsheet on laptops or tablets

ROUND UP!
Groups present their conclusions and explain how the data informed their decision.

ASSESSMENT OPPORTUNITIES
Were children able to:
1. Design a fair test for deciding on the better cup?
2. Use the spreadsheet to record and graph the data?
3. Use their data to make a choice of cup?
4. Present a convincing rationale for their choice of cup?

8.5 Mini enterprise: How much should I charge?

INTRODUCTION

This task invites children put themselves into the situation of generating funds for charity through a mini enterprise. They must decide on a product they wish to make (greetings cards, handicrafts, toffee apples, cakes, *etc*), determine the costs and then decide on how much to sell the product for in order to ensure they have covered all the costs and made money for the charity.

TEACHING SEQUENCE

Overview:

- introduction – how can you raise money for charity?
- preparation – work in groups to decide on a product they could make to sell in order to raise money for charity
- purpose – ensure that what they charge for the product covers costs and raises money for charity
- exploring – find out likely costs for their chosen product – are there any economies of scale? Are there any logistical issues? *eg* cakes would need to be fresh when they are sold
- investigation – enter costs on a spreadsheet and model different pricing scenarios
- extension – what other things might need to be taken into account if you were going to make and sell the product?
- evaluation – present to the class the proposed product and justification for price

➡ A whole class discussion about how charities raise money. You might want to show charity websites

➡ Each group decides on a product to make and sell in order to raise money for charity.

Learning Objective
- To use a spreadsheet model to assist with deciding on the charge to make for a product

Key Vocabulary
- Production costs
- Profit
- Pricing

Resources
- Spreadsheet on laptops or tablets
- Charity catalogues and websites

➡ Groups investigate likely costs and enter these on a spreadsheet so they can determine the cost per product. They can then investigate how much money might be raised by charging different prices.

ROUND UP!

Groups present their chosen product and justify the charge to the rest of the class. It would be an exciting experience for children to actually make their products and sell them.

ASSESSMENT OPPORTUNITIES

Were children able to:

1. Identify different ways that charities raise money?

2. Design a product and identify all the related costs?

3. Enter information on a spreadsheet and explore different costing options?

4. Present their product to the class and justify their chosen price?

Chapter 9

E-Safety and digital citizenship

By Ben Sedman

About this chapter

In this chapter children will learn about the safe and appropriate use of the internet and how to conduct themselves appropriately online (digital citizenship). A range of interactive activities have been included, which can be modified to meet the needs of children in both Key Stage 1 and Key Stage 2. To develop your own knowledge and understanding within this area, it is suggested you complete the online training offered by CEOP www.thinkuknow.co.uk/Teachers/KCSO or become a CEOP Ambassador.

KEY TERMS

E-Safety: the safe and responsible use of technology.

Safeguarding: protecting and keeping ourselves safe online.

Digital literacy: is the ability to find, evaluate, utilize, share, and create content using information technologies and the internet.

CEOP: Child Exploitation and Online Protection.

Content: harm that can arise from exposure to age inappropriate, distasteful or illegal content

Conduct: harm that can arise from how young people behave online

Contact: harm that can arise from interactions with other individuals online.

ACTIVITIES

1. Online Safety
2. Stranger Danger
3. Snakes and Ladders
4. Tablet Spinner

CROSS-CURRICULAR

- Speaking and listening
- PHSET
- Geography
- Design and Technology

USEFUL LINKS

www.ceop.police.uk

www.thinkuknow.co.uk

www.kidsmart.org.uk

www.saferinternet.org.uk

www.childnet.org

www.youtube.com/watch?v=_o8auwnJtqE

www.vimeo.com/channels/insafe2012

Thank you to the primary trainees, at Manchester Metropolitan University, who have also contributed their ideas to help create some of these activities!

9.1 Online safety

INTRODUCTION

To begin with, this activity will demonstrate to the children how people behave differently online and do not always tell the truth. The activity will also highlight how easily it could not be the person you thought it was you were talking to when online. The children will be given the opportunity to watch and evaluate a 'staying safe online' video created by BrainPOP UK. They will then create and produce their own e-safety video. This could be shared with another class, during assembly, on a blog or a school website.

TEACHING SEQUENCE

Overview:

- preparation – questioning and e-safety video
- purpose – identify an audience
- planning – decide on content for own video
- making – create the video
- final outcome – save completed video to the class blog
- evaluation – reflecting on what worked

➡ Encourage the children to ask you, the teacher, questions, (see resource 9.1a).

➡ Sit at the front of the classroom with your back to the children and display your written answers on the interactive whiteboard for the class to see. This will illustrate to the children that it is very difficult to judge if someone is telling the truth when they cannot see that person.

➡ The children will then repeat the activity, in pairs, using a computer or tablet. This will demonstrate how easily it is to lie or be told a lie when using the internet.

➡ The children will watch the e-safety video created by Brainpop (others can be used)

Learning Objective
- To use technology safely, respectfully and responsibly
- Recognise acceptable/unacceptable behaviour online
- Identify a range of ways to report concerns about content and contact

Key Vocabulary
- Respectful
- Responsible
- Acceptable
- Unacceptable
- Produce
- E-safety

Resources
- BrainPop video
- Computers
- Filming devices
- Tablets
- E-Safety Quiz

www.brainpop.co.uk/psheandcitizenship/pshekeepingsafe/onlinesafety

➡ Discuss the rules highlighted. Ask, what makes the video effective? How could they improve the video? (*eg* use a tag line, have a key phrase or involve real people)

- In groups, the children will list the different themes regarding e-safety which are highlighted within the video (*eg* sharing personal data and talking to strangers)

- Next, explain that they have been given the opportunity to create their very own e-safety video which will include some of the themes mentioned in the Brainpop video, except this time they will be the stars!

- Each group will design and create a short video. Refer back to how the video could be improved, include suggested improvements in their video. Individual roles can be allocated to group members (*eg* director, actor and script editor)

- Support the children as they create their videos.

- The completed videos could be uploaded to the class/school blog or website and be part of an e-safety day/week. Videos could be created using Windows Live Movie Maker (see resource 9.1b) or iMovie (see resource 9.1c)

ROUND UP!

Children will watch and evaluate their completed videos. Comment on key messages and themes. If completed as a drama activity and not filmed, freeze frames could be included with directed questions included, for example, what is this character thinking? Why is this character upset?

ASSESSMENT OPPORTUNITIES
Were children able to:
1. think and behave imaginatively?
2. create an original e-safety video?
3. produce an outcome of value in relation to the objective?
4. edit the video content successfully?

5. complete the E-safety quiz (refer to Brainpop link) How has their own knowledge and understanding developed? www.brainpop.co.uk//uk/psheandcitizenship/pshekeepingsafe/onlinesafety/quiz

Resource 9.1a
Example Questions To Ask Your Teacher!

Where do you work?
Do you have any children?
How old are you?
Where do you live?
How do you travel to work?
What do you do after work?
Do you belong to a club?
What sport do you like?
Where do you go on holiday?
What else would you like to find out?

Resource 9.1b
How to use Windows Live Movie Maker

Equipment: A computer (PC or laptop) and film editing software *eg* Microsoft Movie Maker (download for free)
How to use software
1. Click on Start button
2. Click on All Programmes icon
3. Click on Windows Movie Maker icon
4. Click on Import video and find your first scene of animation
5. Drag and drop the scene into the video timeline
6. Click on Import video again and drag and drop other scenes onto your timeline
7. Click on Make titles or credits
8. Choose which type of title you would like to use
9. Click on Make titles or credits again and add titles to your scenes
10. Click on Import audio or music and find your music
11. Click on Import

12. Drag and drop the music onto the Audio/Music timeline
13. Click the Play button to play your film
14. Click Save project button
15. Name your project and click Save
16. Click Finish Movie Choose which type of format you would like to save your film. Follow the instructions to save it

Resource 9.1c

How to use iMovie – iMovie for beginners
www.youtube.com/watch?v=ZGG5kbMKmLo

iMovie Guide
http://iosguides.net/app-guides/imovie-for-ipad/

9.2 Stranger Danger

INTRODUCTION

The main aim of this lesson is for the children to realise how easily it is to be tricked online and to make them aware of how easily people can reveal private information to strangers. The children will access an online **chatroom** via Edmodo. They will be ticked into thinking they are chatting to a child from another school, but it will really be their teacher or another member of staff. After the truth has been revealed, the children will be involved in a discussion, then produce e-safety posters using the PicCollage App

TEACHING SEQUENCE

Overview:

- preparation – chatroom discussion
- purpose – staying safe online
- planning – discussion
- making –create posters
- final outcome – evaluate the posters
- evaluation – reflecting on what worked

➡ Ask a member of staff to introduce the session, explaining that you, the teacher, are unable to take the lesson today. The staff member will introduce the 'fake' learning objective for the lesson. (The learning objective will involve interacting with a student, via a chat room, from another part of the country as part of a geography topic, to find out what it would be like living there).

➡ Give the children a QR code to scan (see resource 9.2a) which will to link the children to a chatroom called Edmodo.

➡ In small groups, the children will log on and start 'chatting'. You, the class teacher, will be in another room asking questions and finding out about the children in the class.

Learning Objective
- To use technology safely, respectfully and responsibly
- Recognise acceptable/ unacceptable behaviour online

Key Vocabulary
- Chatroom
- Responsible
- Acceptable
- Unacceptable

Resources
- Chatroom account
- Edmodo
- iPads
- QR code
- Pic Collage App

➡ You will have a fake profile and photograph of a child, the same age as the children in the class, which you will share with the class.

➡ You will ask leading questions to obtain personal information from the children, for example, where their school is, clubs they attend and any hobbies and interests.

➡ After 20 minutes you will stop chatting, then return to the classroom and ask the children to share the lesson they have been working on. You will then reveal yourself as the 'fake' child that they were chatting to.

➡ Discuss with children how this made them feel. Highlight how easy it is for people to lie online and how they must keep safe online by not sharing any personal information.

ROUND UP!

Using an iPad or tablet, use the PicCollage app (see resource 9.2b) to create an online safety poster. Children can use the discussion to inform their class poster. Posters could also be created on paper.

ASSESSMENT OPPORTUNITIES

Were children able to:

1. think and behave imaginatively when creating the poster?
2. create an original poster?
3. produce an outcome of value in relation to the objective?
4. edit the poster content successfully?

Resource 9.2a

QR Codes

QR stands for Quick Response Code. They are a type of bar code which can store web addresses (URLs). If you install a QR code reader application you will be able to take a picture of the code which will automatically link your device to the web page.

If you are using an Edmodo chat room, create a QR code of the webpage. When the children scan the QR code with their ipad they will be taken straight to the chat room. This will avoid unnecessary searching and will ensure all the children use the same secure chat room. To create a QR code visit www.qrstuff.com They are very quick and easy to create and are incredibly useful!

You could add QR codes to children's work so they can be scanned and provide feedback. Parents could also scan QR codes, using their mobile phones, which are attached to work in your school corridors and will take them to blogs and other useful weblinks.

You can also add QR codes to paper, T-shirts and mugs!

Resource 9.2b

 Using the PicCollage App

Open the App

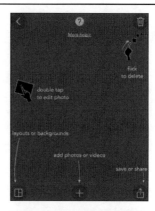

Tap to create a new collage

Add text, photographs, video and different themes. Save and share!

9.3 Snakes and Ladders!

INTRODUCTION

This activity will support the teaching of **e-safety**. The children will be given the opportunity to design, make and evaluate a traditional snakes and ladders game with a twist! Through design and playing the game, the children will learn about e-safety and staying safe online.

TEACHING SEQUENCE

Overview:

- preparation – look at examples
- purpose – identify an audience
- planning – think about the design
- making – create the game
- final outcome – play the completed game
- evaluation –reflect on what worked

➡ Introduce the children to a snakes and ladders board game. Let them play the game. Discuss features (recap concept www.wikihow.com/Play-Snakes-and-Ladders)

➡ Explain that the children will be designing their own version of the board game with a link to e-safety. Explain that their version will be slightly different to the original snakes and ladders board game because when a player lands on a snake or a ladder they will pick up a card and read it out (see resource 9.3a)

➡ Each card is a statement regarding e-safety. If it is a positive e-safety statement, something the children should do, this is a ladder statement and the player will move forward up the ladder. If it is a negative e-safety statement, something the children should not do, the player will move backwards down a snake.

Learning Objective
- To use technology safely, respectfully and responsibly
- Recognise acceptable/unacceptable behaviour online
- Identify a range of ways to report concerns about content and contact

Key Vocabulary
- Respectful
- Responsible
- Acceptable
- Unacceptable
- Produce
- E-safety

Resources
- BrainPop video
- Computers
- Filming devices
- Tablets
- E safety quiz

➡ Give each child a blank snake and ladders board (see resource 9.3b) This could be photocopied on card or A3 paper. Explain to the children that they will need to decorate their board and add their snakes and ladders. Explain that the children could design their own snakes and ladders or use the ones provided (see resource 9.3c).

➡ Give a copy of the snakes and ladders e-safety statements and discuss why there are positive or negative aspects of e-safety. Discuss which statements will keep children safe online. Ask the children to cut the statements out and put in a pile face down. The children could write 'snakes' or 'ladders' on the top of each card. (To differentiate, you could ask children to search for their own statements!)

ROUND UP!

When the board games are completed, provide dice and counters (the children could make their own) and ask the children to play their games. Do this in pairs or small groups. Ask the children to evaluate each other's games. Discuss how playing the games supported their understanding of e-safety. Share the completed board games with other children throughout the school.

ASSESSMENT OPPORTUNITIES

Discuss the work covered.

Were children able to:

1. think and behave imaginatively?
2. create an original board game?
3. produce an outcome of value in relation to the objective?
4. play the board games successfully and develop their understanding of e-safety?

Snake cards

A website asked you for your date of birth when joining. You lied and said you were older than your actual age. **Move down the snake!**

You decide to meet up with someone you have met online. **Never do this! Move down the snake!**

You post your home address on a website so anyone can see it. **Never do that! Move down the snake!**

You befriend people you don't know on a social networking site. **Never do this! Move down the snake!**

You post photographs of your friends and family without their permission on a social networking site. Anyone can download these. **Never do this! Move down the snake!**

Ladder cards

You accidentally come across something inappropriate. You shut down the webpage and tell an adult. **Well done. Move up the ladder!**

A website asked you for your date of birth when joining. You realised you were not old enough to join it and left the site. **Well done. Move up the ladder!**

You keep your password to your online account private and change it if you think someone might know it. **Well done. Move up the ladder!**

You keep your mobile phone number safe and do not share it with anyone on the internet. **Well done. Move up the ladder!**

You receive a nasty message on a site. You report this to an adult and the sender is blocked. **Well done. Move up the ladder!**

Snakes and ladders board

100	99	98	97	96	95	94	93	92	91
81	82	83	84	85	86	87	88	89	90
80	79	78	77	76	75	74	73	72	71
61	62	63	64	65	66	67	68	69	70
60	59	58	57	56	55	54	53	52	51
41	42	43	44	45	46	47	48	49	50
40	39	38	37	36	35	34	33	32	31
21	22	23	24	25	26	27	28	29	30
20	19	18	17	16	15	14	13	12	11
1	2	3	4	5	6	7	8	9	10

Resource 9.3c
Snakes and ladders

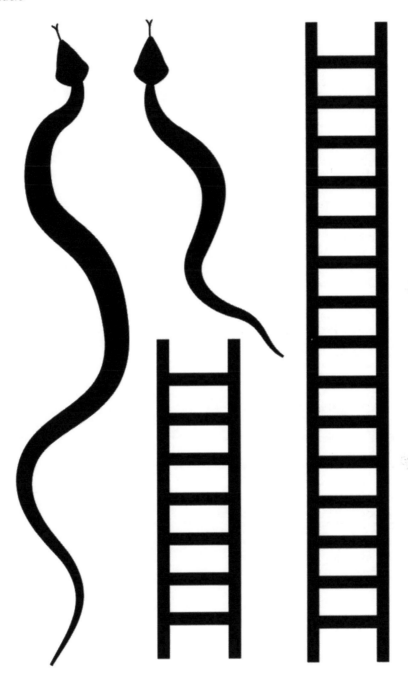

9.4 Tablet spinner

INTRODUCTION
This activity will support the teaching of e-safety. The children will be given the opportunity to design, make and evaluate a spinner for a tablet case. Through designing and using the spinner, the children will learn about e-safety and staying safe online.

TEACHING SEQUENCE
Overview:
- preparation – look at an example
- purpose – identify an audience
- planning – think about the design
- making – create the spinner
- final outcome – spin it!
- evaluation – reflect on what worked

➡ Show the children an example of a spinner on a tablet cover (see resource 9.4a), demonstrate how it works. Pull the lever and the arrows point to the different e-safety statements.

➡ With the children, discuss that they will be creating a similar spinner, which will highlight different aspects of e-safety.

➡ Discuss and make notes with the children regarding information that they will include in the 'Do' (top part) of their spinner cover. (Things they should do to stay safe online)

➡ Repeat discussion for the 'Don't' (bottom part) of their spinner cover. (Things they should not do online)

➡ Let the children create their spinners. Use card, paper fasteners and other resources you may want to use. (see resource 9.4b for a step-by-step guide). Ensure you highlight the key vocabulary on the spinner – fixed

Learning Objective
- To use technology safely, respectfully and responsibly
- Recognise acceptable/ unacceptable behaviour online

Key Vocabulary
- Chatroom
- Responsible
- Acceptable
- Unacceptable

Resources
- Chatroom account
- Edmodo
- iPads
- QR code
- Pic Collage App

and moving pivot and lever. Refer to real life examples.

➡ Attach the lever using a paper faster. Explain when the children pull the lever the spinner will move.

➡ Attach the spinner to the card cover using a paper fastener.

➡ When the spinner is attached to the card cover, ask the children to decorate it and add the e-safety statements. The statements will have been decided during the discussion at the start of the lesson. (see resource 9.4a for examples)

ROUND UP!

➡ Discuss the e-safety statements the children have included. Ask why they think the ones they have included are important.

➡ Discuss the different designs of the spinners created. Discuss which one stands out and why. Ask what improvements they would make if they were to repeat the activity?

➡ Recap pivots and levers.

ASSESSMENT OPPORTUNITIES

Discuss the work covered. Were children able to:
1. think and behave imaginatively?
2. create an original spinner design?
3. produce an outcome of value in relation to the objective?
4. able to use their spinner successfully and develop their understanding of e-safety?

Resource 9.4a
Spinner Tablet Cover

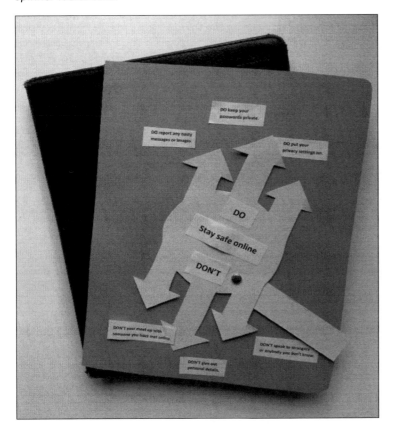

Resource 9.4b
Spinner Instructions

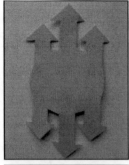

Cut out your spinner design. Use the example here or create your own!

Connect your spinner to your tablet card cover using a paper fastener. (This is a fixed pivot!)

Add a lever. This will make your spinner move when you pull it!

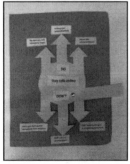

Add your Do's and Don'ts for keeping safe online. Stick it to the cover of your tablet and spin!

Chapter 10

Imagine, write and share: Blogs, wikis and web design

By Ben Sedman

About this chapter

In this chapter children will learn how to write and share information using blogs and wikis. They will be taught about the safe and appropriate use of the internet and how to conduct themselves appropriately online when using a blog or wiki. A range of interactive activities have been included, which can be modified to meet the needs of children in both Key Stage 1 and Key Stage 2.

KEY TERMS

Blog: an example of Web2.0 technology, it is like a website which information is posted to, often in a journal format.

Wiki: an example of Web2.0 technology, it is like a website which anyone can add information to.

Posting comments: If someone has comments enabled on his or her blog, then you can usually find a 'comments' link at the end of each post.

Blogger: a person who has a blog.

RSS Feeds: a file containing a blog's latest posts.

Photoblog: a blog mostly containing photos, posted constantly and chronologically.

Blog design: theme of your blog.

ACTIVITIES

1. Writing your first blog
2. Rainforest animal blog
3. Blog for a famous person
4. Class recipe wiki

CROSS-CURRICULAR

- Literacy
- Speaking and listening
- PHSET
- Geography
- Design and Technology
- Science
- History

USEFUL LINKS

www.kidsblogclub.com

www.simonhaughton.co.uk/blog_index.html

www.kidslearntoblog.com

www.support.google.com/blogger/answer/42399?hl=en

10.1 Writing your first blog: Let's get blogging!

INTRODUCTION

This activity will enable the children to create a **blog**. A blog is an example of Web2.0 technology, it is like a website which information is posted to, often in a journal format. The children will learn how to manipulate, edit and store information on a blog and will be given the opportunity to evaluate a range of blogs and create their own. The completed blogs can be uploaded to the class website for family and friends to access

TEACHING SEQUENCE

Overview:

* preparation – look at and evaluate a range of blogs
* purpose – identify an audience
* planning – decide on content for blog
* making – create the blog
* final outcome – save blog to the internet
* evaluation – reflecting on what worked

➡ Ask the children if they have heard of a blog. Explain what a blog is. A blog is a website that allows groups or individuals to share their work and ideas, as stories, photographs and videos. Blogs also enable users to write comments.

➡ With the children, look at a range of blogs. Discuss the content, for example, blog entries are generally short and appear in reverse chronological order (see resource 10.1a).

➡ E-safety tip: Introduce and discuss the rules for blogging (see resource 10.1b). Ask the children if they could add any other rules to the list.

➡ Introduce a blog which the children will be working on (refer to one of the

Learning Objective
* Understand how to write a blog
* Learn how to manipulate, edit and store a range of media on a blog

Key Vocabulary
* Variety of blogs
* Blogging rules
* Internet
* PCs/tablets

Resources
* Blog
* Manipulate
* Edit
* Store
* Post

recommended blogs below). Discuss the features of the blog chosen (see resource 10.1c for features of Wordpress)

➡ Demonstrate how to upload a written entry to a blog. Explain that it is like a journal entry and could be a review. Discuss that a review can be your opinion of anything, for example, the last good book you read, a meal you ate at a restaurant or a place you visited. Explain that in a review you write about the good bits and the bits that could be improved, what you liked and what you would change.

Ask the children to think about something to blog about. For example, this could be if you could interview your favourite pop star, what would you ask them? What was your best holiday or day out? What makes you happy? What makes you sad? What are your favourite lessons in school and why? The children could draft writing their blog post on paper before posting it. The children could then post their own blog posts.

Recommended Blogs
- Edlogger
- Kidsblog
- Typepad
- Wordpress
- Edublogs
- Blogoshere

ROUND UP!
➡ Share, read and evaluate the blog posts. Discuss how well the information is presented, ask what other forms of media could be embedded within a blog eg photographs and video content.

➡ Discuss how the children coped with writing their own blog entries and ask how they would improve them in future.

Extension task
Demonstrate how to upload photographs and video content to a blog. Allow the children to upload photographs and /or videos to support their blog posts. Refer back to the blogging rules.

Now create your own class blog
This could include:
- Children being responsible for adding content eg work completed during lessons, homework activities, QR codes and school trips.

- Promoting work taking place in schools eg videos of celebration assemblies, photographs of displays and clubs.
- Posting local and national news and things children find interesting and would want to share with others.
- Having a class blogger of the day or week.
- Tweeting about your blog!

ASSESSMENT OPPORTUNITIES
Were children able to:
1. think and behave imaginatively?
2. create an original blog post?
3. produce an outcome of value in relation to the objective?
4. edit the blog content successfully?

Resource 10.1a
What makes a good blog?
Think about:
What is your blog about? Educational, about a hobby or interest?
Who is your audience? Friends, family, or children at school?
How will you make it readable? Will it be presented in sections? Include short posts? Font colour and layout.
How will you make sure it is the right length? Could you ask someone to proof read it to check for any mistakes?
How will you grab a reader's attention? Think about using titles and the use of colour. Could you include intriguing statements and catchy phrases?
How will you make your blog engaging? Could you use pictures and video content? Include links to other websites.
Could you ask your readers to do things? Could visitors leave a comment or click on a link?
Can we think of any other features we would want to include?

Resource 10.1b

Blogging Rules!

1. Just display your first name and not your surname on your blog
2. Keep your personal details private *eg* email, phone number, email and home or school address
3. Always keep your password safe and don't tell others what it is
4. Never post anything that is rude or upsetting
5. Always ask permission if you write anything about someone
6. Only post your own work to your blog
7. Only use your username and password

Resource 10.1c

Features of Wordpress

1. Very simple to use when wanting to publish your own website and content
2. Flexibility: allows you to create any type of website. For example, a personal blog, website or a photoblog
3. Add a range of plugins and themes to make the website unique
4. Very easy to publish. Just click a button and the content becomes live
5. Allows others (friends or family) to manage and add content to your website
6. Lots of fun tools to help you upload pictures, videos, captions text *etc*
7. Built in comments allows friends and family to add comments to your content
8. Multilingual – available in more than 70 languages!

For further information visit https://wordpress.org/about/features/

10.2 Rainforest blog

INTRODUCTION

This activity will enable the children to create a **blog** about an animal or group of animals living in the rainforest. The stimulus could be a book about the rainforest, *eg* The Great Kapok Tree: A Tale of the Amazon Rain Forest by Lynne Cherry. The children will carry out **research** about the animal(s) and using the information collected, will create a blog containing information about the animal(s). When completed, the blogs will be shared so others can post **comments** and find out about the animal. The children will compose a comment from the point of view of the animal.

TEACHING SEQUENCE

Overview:

*   preparation – look at blog examples
*   purpose – identify an audience
*   planning – decide on animal(s) to research
*   making – research the animal(s)
*   final outcome – create and post blog
*   evaluation – reflecting on what worked

➡ Read the book *The Great Kapok Tree: A Tale of the Amazon Rain Forest* by Lynne Cherry (or a similar book as a stimulus). This book is set in the Brazilian rainforest and introduces the children to importance of trees and how 'all living things depend on one another'. This YouTube video can also be used if the book is not available https://www.youtube.com/watch?v=gw0arFtHeVw

➡ Discuss the different types of animals introduced to the children. Discuss what makes them special and their characteristics.

➡ Give each child one or a group of the rainforest animals introduced to them in the book to research.

Learning Objective

*   Create a blog about an animal from the rainforest
*   Upload text, photographs and video content

Key Vocabulary

*   Blog
*   Research
*   Post
*   Comments
*   Edit

Resources

*   The Great Kapok Tree: A Tale of the Amazon Rain Forest
*   Computer
*   Internet
*   Blog

➡ Discuss where this information could be stored for others to view. Explain that they are going to create their own blog about that particular animal or group of animals.

➡ Refer to the following examples: www.livingrainforest.org/kids http://kids.mongabay.com

- Discuss the features of the blog (see resources Features of a Blog 10.1a and Blogging Rules 10.1b)

- Children can begin to create their blogs. Ensure they include different features of a blog and refer to the blogging rules.

- Remind and demonstrate how to upload photographs and video content.

ROUND UP!

Share completed blogs. Evaluate each other's work. Discuss what worked well and what they would improve. Could they include photographs and video content?

Ask the children to compose a comment to post on another blog. Could they write a comment from the point of view of the animal?

ASSESSMENT OPPORTUNITIES

Were children able to:

1. think and behave imaginatively?
2. create an original blog post?
3. produce an outcome of value in relation to the objective?
4. edit the blog content successfully?
5. ask and answer a question posted on a blog?

10.3 Blog for a famous person!

INTRODUCTION

This activity will enable the children to create a **blog** about a famous person (This could be linked to any topic being covered in school, for example, The Tudors and Henry VIII). The children will carry out **research** about the person and using the information collected, will create a blog containing information about the person. When completed, the blogs will be shared so others can **post comments** and find out about the famous person. The children could post comments pretending they are that particular person, for example, Henry VIII could contact Julius Caesar and Robin Hood could contact Queen Elizabeth I.

TEACHING SEQUENCE

Overview:

- preparation – look at blog examples
- purpose – identify an audience
- planning – decide on a famous person
- making – research the famous person
- final outcome – create and post blog
- evaluation – reflecting on what worked

➡ Give each child a famous person to research *eg* Henry VIII. Collect useful information including photographs and videos. Begin to write up important information. Tell the children that this is written like a journal.

➡ The teacher will demonstrate/recap how to write a blog (see resource 10.1a)

➡ **E-safety tip:** Refer to blogging rules, can you think of other rules to include? (see resource 10.1b)

➡ Each child will create their own blog about a famous person.

➡ Once the blogs have been created:

Learning Objective
- Create a blog
- Ask questions and add comments to a blog

Key Vocabulary
- Blog
- Research
- Edit
- Post
- comments

Resources
- Blog
- Computer/tablet
- Internet

1. In pairs, the children will peer assess each other's blogs. The teacher will encourage the children to check for any punctuation or grammatical errors.
2. Discuss what makes a good post or comment (see resource 10.3a).
3. The teacher will choose a blog and demonstrate how to join in a discussion.
4. Allow the children to draft what they would write before they type in their entry.
5. Allow time for the students to type their blog entries.

6. Students respond to another student's blog entry.

ROUND UP!

In role, children pretend to be the person they have researched and written a blog about. They will answer the questions, which have been posted on their blog in the role of the famous person.

Extension Activity

Ask the children to embed 'Padlet' and 'Voicethread' on to their blogs. Discuss how these could be used to enhance their blogs.

Padlet is a virtual wall that allows people to express their thoughts on a shared topic. https://padlet.com

Voicethread is a web-based application that allows people have conversations and make comments using any mix of a microphone, a web cam, a telephone or an audio file. https://voicethread.com

ASSESSMENT OPPORTUNITIES

Were children able to:
1. think and behave imaginatively?
2. create an original blog post?
3. produce an outcome of value in relation to the objective?
4. edit the blog content successfully?
5. ask and answer a question posted on a blog?

Resource 10.3a

Writing quality comments
- Using the correct punctuation, spelling and spacing
- Read over and check your comment before submitting it
- Complementing the writer
- Adding a question about the post
- Adding new information relevant to the post in your comment *eg* a useful web link
- Not including personal information in your comment

10.4 Class recipe wiki

INTRODUCTION

This activity will enable the children to create a wiki. A wiki is an example of **Web2.0** technology, it is like a website anyone can add to. The best example is Wikipedia, the online encyclopaedia that allows anyone to add and edit its entries. The children will learn how to **manipulate**, **edit** and **store** information on a wiki to create an online recipe resource. The children will be given the opportunity to evaluate a range of wikis and create their own. The completed class recipe wiki could be shared on a class blog or website for family and friends to access.

TEACHING SEQUENCE

Overview:

- preparation – look at wiki examples
- purpose – identify an audience
- planning – decide on favourite recipe
- making – cooking/baking – filming, photographing, writing
- final outcome – upload recipe ideas to the wiki
- evaluation – reflecting on what worked

➡ The teacher will evaluate a range of wikis. Discuss content and how they are arranged. Discuss what works well and what does not. (see resource 10.4a)

➡ Either create a class wiki (everyone contributes to the same wiki) or split the class into small groups. Give each group member a role, for example, a WikiChampion – a pupil who can train others to help them get started using a wiki, a WikiBuilders – those who add text, photographs, videos and podcasts, a WikiDesigner – someone who makes the format look good/appealing, and a WikiAssessor – someone who evaluates the wiki.

Learning Objective
- Learn how to manipulate, edit and store a range of media on a wiki

Key Vocabulary
- Web 2.0
- Manipulate
- Store
- Edit
- Wiki

Resources
- Chosen wiki
- Videoing devices
- Digital cameras
- Internet

➡ Explain that the children will each record their favourite recipe (This could be linked to a topic eg healthy eating in D&T or Science). They could search for their recipe on the internet or bring it from home.

➡ Having previously joined a wiki (see recommended free wikis below). The teacher will invite the children to join the wiki via email (each child will click on the link to accept in the email. The teacher should demonstrate this to the class first).

- E-Safety tip: Explain to the children that they must not accept invitations via email unless they have been told to do so by a parent or teacher. (see resource 10.4b Wiki Rules!)

- After demonstrating how to accept the invitation to join the wiki, the teacher will demonstrate how to write up a recipe using a wiki template. When using for educational purposes you can often have advertisement free wiki pages.

- The children will upload and save their recipes to the wiki. Give the children the opportunity to upload this as written information, photographs, videos or using a combination of different media. For example, the children could create their favourite dish and photograph it or film, as they bake or create it!

- As new pages on a wiki are created, the navigation bar grows and the content gets organised.

ROUND UP!
- The teacher will demonstrate how links to the wiki can be emailed or added to other websites. The children can copy and send the link to family members.

- Evaluate the class wiki. Discuss content, what works well? How could they improve it further?

Free wikis
1. Wikispaces
2. PBwiki
3. Wetpaint
4. GlosterED

ASSESSMENT OPPORTUNITIES
Were children able to:
1. think and behave imaginatively?
2. create an original wiki?
3. produce an outcome of value in relation to the objective?
4. edit the wiki content successfully?

Wiki examples:
http://connectingclassroomswithchina.wikispaces.com/home

https://wilbury-minecraft-ancient-egypt.wikispaces.com

Resource 10.4a
Evaluating a Wiki
Discuss the following:
1. What is the published content on this wiki?
2. What catches your eye about this wiki?
3. Is the content easy to read?
4. What types of media are embedded within this wiki?
5. Is there an interesting variety of media embedded within the wiki?
6. How can you check the validity of the data? (How do you know if the information is reliable?)
7. How can you edit this wiki?
8. How can anyone edit this wiki?
9. How could you improve the layout?
10. Is it easy to post comments?

Resource 10.4b
Wiki Rules!!
1. Just display your first name and not your surname on your wiki
2. Keep your personal details private *eg* email, phone number, email, home or school address
3. Always keep your password safe and don't tell others what it is
4. Never post anything that is rude or upsetting
5. Always ask permission if you write anything about someone
6. Only post your own work to your wiki
7. Only use your username and password
8. Any other rules we could add?

Chapter 11

Transition to Secondary: Mapping your skills

By Ellie Overland

About this chapter

In this chapter children will learn to develop their skills from visual methods of programming using Scratch through to text based programming using Python. A 'stepping stone' of Logo provides an option to allow a more scaffolded transition from one to the other.

These lessons are designed to involve some level of communication with a local secondary school. Whilst this is not essential, any level of communication during the transition from year 6 to year 7 can only be beneficial, both to the primary teachers and those in the secondary setting, but most of all to ensure the enjoyment and progress of the pupils.

KEY TERMS

Algorithm: a set of precise instructions to solve a problem or achieve a goal.

Sequence: a set of events or instructions that must be carried out in a specific order within an algorithm.

Selection: is all about decision making, which comes as an outcome of asking questions.

Debugging: identifying and removing errors from scripts and programs.

Testing: a way of checking a program works and does all the things correctly that it was designed to do.

Loops: a sequence of instructions that are repeated until a specific task is achieved.

ACTIVITIES

1. Map it out!
2. Test it out!
3. From blocks to text
4. Turtle activities in Python
5. My Python Map

CROSS-CURRICULAR

- The map it out activity has direct links with geography, particularly different scales of maps and floor plans.
- The testing elements of the chapter require literacy skills, particularly comprehension, to breakdown the problem and list associated success criteria.
- The Logo and Python activities link to mathematics, particularly an understanding of angles and measure.
- Where links have been made with a secondary school through the blog, learners are required to develop their communication skills and consider aspects of digital literacy.

USEFUL LINKS

www.scratch.mit.edu

www.turtleacademy.com

www.kidblog.org/home/

www.python.org/downloads

11.1 Map it out!

INTRODUCTION

Before starting this unit it is useful for the students to have already made contact with a secondary school as pupils or staff at the new school could set the challenges and place the problem in a real context. Kidblog is one way this could be done to allow communication and comments in a secure and moderated environment.

In this lesson, the students will identify their task from the digital communications they have been sent. This could be to get from their home to the new school, to get from the shops, bus stop or other specified location to the school or to navigate between the classrooms in their new school. The lesson builds on prior knowledge developed in using Scratch. To place this lesson in a wider computational context, ask pupils to think about the prospect of self driving cars and how these might work. Also to think about how robots are used now within warehouses to move and collect items. An interesting video is here: www.youtube.com/watch?v=UtBa9yVZBJM

Learning Objective
- Select and combine digital content
- Design and write programs that accomplish specific goals

Key Vocabulary
- Sequence
- Skew
- Stretch
- Efficiency

Resources
- Blog
- Scratch program
- Digital map/floor plan

TEACHING SEQUENCE

➡ The challenge of navigation is explained to the students either by their teacher or, preferably via digital communications from their new school. This could be the format of a video message or written communication *eg* a blog post

➡ Students to add map/floor plan as a background in Scratch

➡ Students to consider scale of map/plan and create an appropriate sized sprite

➡ Students to read their digital communications and list the challenges they need their sprite to complete (*eg* walk to the front entrance of school from the bus stop)

➡ Students to use the 'pen' blocks to create a program for their sprite to complete each challenge. To extend, routes could become more complex, involving subroutines such as a detour to the park (map) or the canteen (floor plan)

ROUND UP!

Discuss how the problems were tackled *eg* identify the start and end points. Ask the class to share any problems they had when writing their scripts and the strategies that they used to develop their routes. Have they successfully completed the challenge set?

ASSESSMENT OPPORTUNITIES

➡ Ask the students to take either a screenshot or a photo of their navigation solutions and then explain the steps they went through.

➡ Explanation and screen shots to be added to the blog for feedback from their new school (wherever possible).

FIG 1 Blog post example

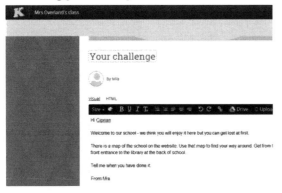

STEP 1: Identify the task

- Read the digital communication and list the task(s).
- Find and save an appropriate map/plan to be used in the Scratch project.

STEP 2: Import the background

- Import background to new Scratch project.
- Consider the scale and positioning of the map. Take care not to **skew** or **stretch** the map.
- Select (or import) an appropriate sprite who will be the navigator. Resize them to an appropriate scale for the map.

FIG 2 Screen shot to show import background

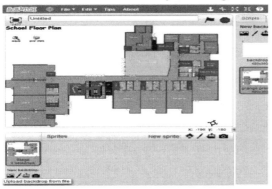

STEP 3: Add script to navigator sprite

- Use the control and pen blocks to create a script to move your navigator from the start point to the destination.
- Have you followed the shortest route? How do you know?
- Consider what will happen when they get there. Will they go somewhere else or back to the start? How can you reverse the route **efficiently**? Will each route be drawn in a different colour?

FIG 3 Screen shot to show sample code to draw navigator route

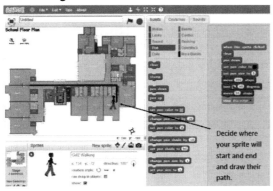

Decide where your sprite will start and end and draw their path.

Time to check and discuss

- Does your sprite take an efficient route and successfully reach the destination.
- Does your sprite always return to a single starting point or do different scripts take it to different destinations?
- How have you dealt with obstacles such as stairs or road crossings? Does your sprite pause or jump?

11.2 Test it out!

INTRODUCTION

Ideally this lesson will be combined with a visit to their new school or a walk near their new schools to familiarise themselves with the new environment. If this is not possible, the code could be tested by students at the secondary school and they could report back via digital communications.

In this lesson students will test the code they developed in activity 1. They will not make use of the visual image of the map/plan but will focus on the code itself.

TEACHING SEQUENCE

➡ Initially the students need to calculate the scale of their map/plan within Scratch to be able to test it in the 'real world'.

➡ Students to take paper copies of their code and follow it in the real environment.

➡ Students to consider the success of the scale of their code in the real environment and situations the 2D map/plan missed *eg* crossing roads, stairs, doors *etc.*

➡ Students consider if the route they coded is the most efficient or were there alternatives they missed?

➡ The code is tested in the real world and students then return to Scratch to modify and develop efficiency in code.

ROUND UP!

Discuss why computational solutions need to be tested. Collate the issues and improvements they identified through their testing process.

Learning Objective
- Apply computational code in real life situations
- Test and modify computational code

Key Vocabulary
- Scale
- Test
- Modify
- Efficiency

Resources
- Paper copy of Scratch code from activity 1
- Meter rulers/Trundle wheels

ASSESSMENT OPPORTUNITIES

➡ The students can take photos or videos of their 'real world' testing.

➡ Their findings and modifications can be written up on the blog along with screen shots of updated code.

STEP 1: Calculate the scale

- Students predict the scale of their Scratch code *eg* what unit of measure does 'forward 1' represent on their map (1 meter, 1 footstep, 30cm *etc*)
- Students select an appropriate tool to make measurements in the real world and see if their prediction is correct.
- Once they have calculated correctly, they are ready to test their code.

STEP 2: Test the code

- Students follow their code exactly as prescribed and note down any issues *eg* inaccuracies (distance and angles), potential obstacles, inefficient routes *etc* in order to test each route.
- Using their 'real world' testing they note down any modifications they need to make to their code to improve it.
- They return to their original code from activity 1 and make the modifications.

STEP 3: Explaining the modifications

- Students use their blog, or other digital communications, to report on their testing. They need to develop a systematic approach to presenting this.
- Students explain what their 'real world' testing found that their onscreen actions did not show.

Time to check and discuss

- Are you happy with the scale of your program? How could you modify this?
- Is your map/plan a true representation of the 'real world'?
- Have you found it useful to test in a 'real world' situation? Why?
- How could this process help you in now writing a new program for a different route or location?

11.3 From blocks to text

INTRODUCTION

Many secondary schools will introduce students to text based programming languages early on in Key Stage 3. It is important students are able to make the connections between their prior learning and new ways of working. Where connections are made clear, progression to text based programming need not be daunting. This lesson moves pupils from physical computing to on screen using Logo. Some teachers may find this step unnecessary for their students and move them directly into Python (activity 4).

TEACHING SEQUENCE

➡ Students revise work with roamers/Bee-Bots and link it to activities 1 and 2.

➡ Students consider what would happen if the Bee-Bot commands were added to Scratch to control a sprite and vice versa so recognizing that each programming language has its own syntax.

➡ Students try out Logo programming language as a tool and see how to draw shapes and patterns.

Learning Objective
- Use text based commands to control a turtle
- Use angles and distance measures to draw different shapes

Key Vocabulary
- Syntax
- Test
- Modify
- Efficiency

Resources
- Bee-Bots/roamers
- On screen version of Logo

ROUND UP!

Discuss why computational solutions need to be tested. Collate the issues and improvements they identified through their testing process.

ASSESSMENT OPPORTUNITIES

➡ Students can video their Bee-Bots/roamers completing the maze and add a code based commentary over the top.

➡ They can annotate their code using #comments to show how they have developed drawing shapes in Logo. Screen recordings with voice-overs provide an alternative to writing if required.

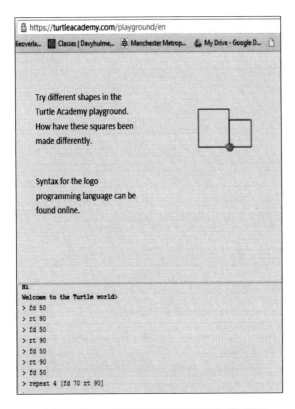

STEP 1: From floor to screen
➡ A maze or route is set out on the floor and students use roamers or Bee-Bots to move through it. Students write down the commands they use.

➡ Students then move to on screen Logo to see how the text based syntax operates.

➡ There are many different versions of Logo available. www.turtleacademy.com. Turtle Academy is free and web based so allows anyone to use it. It also has an exciting gallery of projects to allow pupils to see other creative ideas.

STEP 2: Drawing shapes and designs
➡ Students start with drawing simple shapes in Logo including squares and rectangles.

➡ Students can be challenged to try shapes without right angles. They can also be introduced to the repeat command and divide operator to try more challenging shapes.
eg REPEAT 6 [FD 50 RT 360/4]

STEP 3: Challenging each other
➡ Students devise challenges for each other to complete in Turtle Academy. These could be different shapes, patterns or mazes *eg* draw a set of stairs.

➡ Students experiment with changing colours using 'SETPC' followed by a number. This element can be added to the peer challenges.

Time to check and discuss
- How do the commands on screen compare with the Bee-Bot/ roamer?
- Did you find limitations when using Logo? What did you want to do but couldn't? Do you think there is a coding way around this?
- Have you noticed any similarities between using Logo and drawing the route for your sprite in Scratch?

11.4 Turtle Activities in Python

INTRODUCTION
This is many students first introduction to Python although many will come across it often in secondary school. By using the turtle import this provides a visual introduction even though the commands are text based. These activities make use of Python version 3 onwards. It is free to download from www.python.org/downloads

TEACHING SEQUENCE
➡ Students draw simple shapes in Python as previously done in Logo.

➡ Students consider the differences between the commands in Python, Logo and Scratch. How can they get them all to do the same thing *eg* draw a square?

➡ Students try different challenges in Python to produce shapes and patterns.

➡ Students annotate their work using #comments.

ROUND UP!
Discuss why text based programming is used. Does it look familiar? Where else may students have seen something that looks similar? Is it as easy to read as sentences or paragraphs? Why?

ASSESSMENT OPPORTUNITIES
➡ The students can save each shape as a separate program.

➡ Different programs can then be combined to create a picture.

➡ #comments can be used to annotate code and explain their code.

Learning Objective
- Develop text based programming techniques in Python
- Experiment with different code to find solutions to problems

Key Vocabulary
- Syntax
- Text based programming

Resources
- Python IDEo

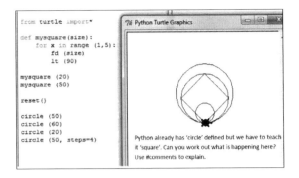

```
from turtle import*

def mysquare(size):
    for x in range (1,5):
        fd (size)
        lt (90)

mysquare (20)
mysquare (50)

reset()

circle (50)
circle (60)
circle (20)
circle (50, steps=4)
```

Python already has 'circle' defined but we have to teach it 'square'. Can you work out what is happening here? Use #comments to explain.

```
from turtle import*
pensize (5)
shape  ("turtle")
lt  (90)
fd  (100)
lt  (90)
fd  (100)
lt  (90)
fd  (100)
lt  (90)
fd  (100)

reset ()

#this code draws a square.
#can you change it to draw a rectangle
```

DESIGN STEPS

STEP 1: Draw simple shapes
➡ Students start off drawing simple shapes such as squares and rectangles.
➡ Using #comments, students annotate their code to show what each line of code does.

STEP 2: Develop more complex shapes
➡ Students follow their code exactly as prescribed and note down any issues *eg* inaccuracies (distance and angles), potential obstacles, inefficient routes *etc* in order to test each route.

➡ Using their 'real world' testing they note down any modifications they need to make to their code to improve it.

➡ They return to their original code from activity 1 and make the modifications.

STEP 3: Challenging each other
➡ Students use their blog, or other digital communications, to report on their testing. They need to develop a systematic approach to presenting this.

➡ Students explain what their 'real world' testing found that their onscreen actions did not show

Time to check and discuss
- Are you happy with the scale of your program? How could you modify this?
- Is your map/plan a true representation of the 'real world'?
- Have you found it useful to test in a 'real world' situation? Why?
- How could this process help you in now writing a new program for a different route or location?

11.5 My Python Map

INTRODUCTION
This lesson requires collaboration, but pupils are not to share images, only the code. They return to the floor plan or map they used in activity 1 and make use of Python code to write their route. The code is tested by other pupils 'on site' to see if it works. Pupils will need to find an efficient way of sharing and commenting on code.

TEACHING SEQUENCE
➡ Students look at their task from activity 1 and consider how it would look without visual elements including the sprite and the plan (stage).

➡ Students transfer their visual task from activity 1 to a text based task in Python. They could explore different destinations and routes to extend their work.

➡ Students use a collaborative, online tool to share their code.

➡ Other students test their code and provide feedback.

ROUND UP!
Discuss why other people may want to test your code. Is it easier to make mistakes in text based code rather than visual?

ASSESSMENT OPPORTUNITIES
➡ Students use #comments in Python to annotate their code to show and explain what it does.

Learning Objective
- Apply computational code in real life situations
- Collaborate to test text only code.

Key Vocabulary
- Syntax
- Test
- Collaborate

Resources
- Python
- Blog, or other online collaborative tool
- Plan/map from activity 1

➡ Feedback from other students allows them to demonstrate successes in their code and make improvements in their work.

➡ A final evaluation can compare the visual and text based approaches.

STEP 1: Plan the route

➡ Students use the original plan/map to plan their route and destinations. They consider the scale they will use for distance in Python compared to distance in the real world.

➡ To develop true collaboration the tasks could be set by the other students who are going to test and feedback.

➡ Once they have planned the route they start producing it in Python using the turtle commands from activity 4.

STEP 2: Collaborate for testing

➡ Students send their code to others for testing.
➡ They could consider the benefits and limitations of sending the Python file itself or just sending the text. What problems might occur?
➡ The testing students follow the text based code to see if it works in the real world. They need to have an understanding of the Python syntax and walk it through in real life rather than view on screen.

STEP 3: Feedback and improvements

➡ The testing students use their online space to provide feedback on the code. If they have sent the Python file they can use #comments to add detail or they could just provide descriptions through the online forum.

➡ The original coders respond to the feedback if required. Once improvements have been made they could send their code through again for further feedback.

➡ Video testing may be an exciting addition here with the testers filming as they walk through the code.

Time to check and discuss

- Was this harder or easier than doing the visual code?
- How easy were the testing comments to understand?
- What did you need to improve and why?
- What apps or software do you think might make use of this type of coding?

Chapter 12

A brief overview of monitoring, evaluating and assessing computing

By Yasemin Allsop

This chapter will provide a brief overview of how to monitor, evaluate and assess computing in link to the activities that are included in this book. Chapter 13 will include more in-depth information about planning and assessment of computing and computational thinking.

Assessment is an integral part of learning and should be tailored to match the schools approach to curriculum organization. Each school will teach computing concepts through different tasks, in different contexts, according to their learners' needs, therefore, it is very difficult to create an assessment scheme that would fit into every schools' curricula.

For many years we used level descriptors, I can statements and even some generic software as an assessment tool to evaluate children's learning in ICT. In the new Computing Curriculum, level descriptors have disappeared. Although this places teachers in an uncertain loop, in terms of assessing computing, it also provides an opportunity to re-think their approaches to assessment in computing.

Level descriptors were structured clearly and were a quick way of checking to see if the children had achieved something, nevertheless, it did not provide opportunities to track pupils' progress or inform children about how they were doing. We used the term 'achieved something' instead of 'learned something' because we do not see learning as only completing a task or a finished work, rather a process of inventing, developing and applying learning behaviours through designing and creating artifacts. This means the assessment of learning that occurs during a computational activity should:

- Be motivational
- Be continuous
- Be personalised
- Be sustainable
- Be evidence based
- Provide opportunities for self and peer assessment

- Support learners to monitor their own learning (meta cognitive awareness)
- Help learners know how to improve
- Provide opportunities for reflection, feedback and celebrating
- Be flexible enough to use in different contexts and different tools
- Provide a system of tracking progression
- Be used to inform planning and identify the next steps

The list above might make people think that assessment in computing was a complex process, however, it is all about making it an integral part of the classroom practice. The aim is not only for the teacher to find out what a student can do, but helping pupils to monitor and reflect on their own learning, so that they are active participants of the learning journey. This should also make learning more meaningful for both learners and teachers. We need to remind ourselves that the core of the assessment in computing is the student, not the technology or the context.

Transferable skills
When we think about assessing children's knowledge and understanding, it is important to look at other invaluable skills the children may develop, which are transferable to any area of learning such as; communication, creativity, critical thinking, advanced technology skills and working collaboratively. In our experience the coding and the game design process itself represents the aspects of creativity where the children use their ideas and imagination to make games. So the assessment process should have a wider focus than subject specific objectives. We should look at how well the students work collaboratively, how

effectively they communicate and the strategies they use, for solving problems. We should also award pupils with badges for demonstrating each of these qualities, as this would shape the interaction, between both the students and the between students and teachers. This interaction will certainly have an impact on pupils learning experience and learning outcome.

Our approach to assessment in computing

We suggest creating individual statements from the programmes of study and using these with badges to provide instant feedback and celebrating achievement. *Computing in the national curriculum: A guide for primary teachers* by Miles Berry provides a detailed treasury of individual statements that can either be used for tracking pupil's attainment or you can always create your own repository according to your curriculum design. The document can be accessed at: www.computingatschool.org.uk/data/uploads/CASPrimaryComputing.pdf

One of the important elements of this approach is to provide instant feedback to students, through the use of either digital or paper badges. This would help the students to monitor their progress, be aware of what they have achieved and what the next steps are. This would only work if every single teacher had training in 'Planning, teaching and assessing computing' as pupils would not only work on a computational activity in the computing lesson but across the curriculum. Additionally, the teachers need to have a secure subject knowledge of the Computing Curriculum and they need to be aware of:

- How to set clear objectives
- What to expect from learners
- How to recognise progress and achievement
- How to identify the skills, knowledge and understanding gained by pupils
- How to support learners to move onto the next step if needed
- Ways of collecting evidence

- How to interpret the evidence to form a judgement and inform their practice

Collecting evidence

There are many ways of collecting evidence of children's work depending on the schools IT infrastructure and available equipment. Students can:

- Use tablets to make a film or take a picture of theirs or their friends activities. Especially recording their discussions are extremely useful to find out about the process of their problem solving activities.
- Use apps such as 'Explain Everything' or Apple 'Pages and Keynote' to annotate their completed work.
- Use Web 2 tools to keep a record of their activities and write about the steps they went through, to complete their work using different multimedia. They can also leave comments on others work and be involved in online discussions to deepen their thinking.
- Create a class wiki using sites such as Wikispaces to upload their work and then write about their design, tinkering and computational thinking processes, to discuss problems that they had and how they designed solutions to overcome these.

Examples:

www.wilbury-minecraft-ancient-egypt.wikispaces.com
www.fortyhallminecraftproject.wikispaces.com
www.gettechnofit.weebly.com/index.html

A simple assessment model

We are aware that we cannot provide a full assessment scheme in this book however we would like to explain briefly how we would assess the learning in the activities that we have shared in Chapters 2 – 11.

- Create a poster of individual statements that will describe the learning for each activity and a badge for students to collect when they met their objectives (See figure 12.1 overleaf for an example) and display it in the classroom. Identify some next steps statements for the children to work towards after collecting a badge, similar to extension or challenges, however it works better if these statements are created collaboratively between the teacher and pupil according to their individual learning needs. Involving children in the design of badges and the name of the badges and even having a competition in the school to create badges makes it really an exciting event for everyone.

- Provide each child with a record sheet where they can keep all of the badges that they have collected (figure 12.2). Place all the statements for the specific age group on their record sheet and a shaded version of their badges so that they know the targets that they need to focus on for the whole year. One reason for this is that students may complete a task in a school club or at home that could earn them a badge, this way we would extend their learning beyond the school walls. Some schools have VLE's that they can award their learners with a digital version of badges, which is very good, but we found that some young children really liked having a little booklet that can be carried around to celebrate their achievements. Using Web 2 tools such as Weebly, Kidsblogs or Wikispaces also can be used for children to set up their own online space where they can collect badges not only for what they have learned in the classroom but also for their online activities. The method of keeping a record of badges collected will depend on the availability of the tools in schools.

- When a pupil moves to a new class, they can take a record of their badges with them

and share it with their new teacher. This would not only help teachers with their planning, but also support them to design personalised learning experiences for their pupils. It also helps the students to manage their own learning so that they can be aware of their own gaps and strengths.

- It is very important to showcase pupils' work and celebrate their achievements with other pupils and parents through the whole school assemblies, class shows and online platforms. Students should learn to be analytical about their own and others work and provide constructive feedback to their peers. They should also learn to take criticism and use the given feedback to improve their work.

- Having a vocabulary section on pupils recording sheet will help them to keep record of the vocabulary that they have learnt during the sessions and also revisit difficult terms, as they need. One way of assessing children's learning in computing is to observe their problem solving activities as it would provide us with a detailed account of their learning process and applying skills. The main difficulty is how we can observe the child's mind and take an image of their mental activities, as thinking is not always visible. There are different ways we can encourage students to share what happens in their mind during the problem solving process. They can explain this by writing on their record sheet or drawing a picture, even using a voice recorder to record their explanations. Teachers can use this knowledge to identify the strategies pupils were able to use and define the cognitive resources that they had developed. This would be very useful in terms of identifying the next steps for the pupils and planning effective learning experiences.

Figure 12.1

Computing Targets

Statement	Badge	Relevant Chapter
I can select and use technology for a particular purpose.	 Tech Star 1	2
I can recognise technology used in school.	 Tech Star2	2
I know what algorithms are	 Algorithm Machine	3, 4, 5, 8, 11
I can create simple programs that accomplish specific goals	 Computer Master 1	3, 4, 8, 11
I can use sequence, selection and repeat in programs	 Computer Master 2	3, 4, 8, 11

I can use variables in programs	Super Computer	3
I can use different software to accomplish given goals	Software wizard 1	6, 5, 10, 11
I can use different applications to create and manipulate digital content	Software wizard 2	5, 6, 7, 8, 10
I can use different tools and applications to collect and present information	Software wizard 3	7, 8
I can use technology safely, in a responsible way	E-safety Coach	9

I can recognize common uses of technology beyond school	Tech Quest	6, 9, 10
I can debug errors in programs	Prof Debug	3, 4, 8, 11
I can use logical reasoning to predict the behaviour of simple programs	Brain Bot	3, 4, 8, 11

Figure 12.2 Print double sided onto card.

My yearly targets are:

-
-
-
-
-

Vocabulary BOX

Write down all the words that you have
learned inside the box

MY COMPUTING PROGRESS LOG

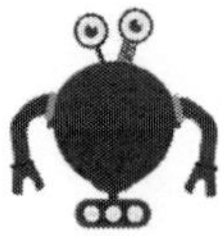

Name:

Start Date:

My individual targets are:

		Date set & Date achieved
①		
②		
③		

MY BADGES

PROBLEM SOLVING

Draw or describe your problem and
explain how you solved it.

My problem was:

This is how I solved it:

_____
_____
_____
_____
_____

Chapter 13

Planning and assessment of computing and computational thinking

By Mark Dorling & John Woollard

Recent years have seen assessment levels abolished and a slimmed down National Curriculum programme of study of just two pages for Key Stages 1, 2 and 3 (ages 5 to 14) introduced. To ensure positive outcomes for our learners there are three important considerations: a correct and shared interpretation of the breadth and depth of the curriculum; a shared understanding of the concepts and what progression looks like; and a clear process for planning and assessment.

What's the major curriculum change?

At the heart of the new statutory programme of study is computational thinking. The opening paragraph of the English National Curriculum for computing says:

'A high quality computing education equips pupils to use computational thinking and creativity to understand and change the world.'

Computational thinking is an activity that occurs in all aspects of the computing curriculum. It should be considered whenever computing lessons are planned and learners' attainment and progression assessed.

The subject association is CAS – Computing At School – and provides leadership, support and direction for this new area of the curriculum – computing.

How do these changes affect the classroom?

Computing's origins lie in philosophy and asking the question 'Why?'. Guidance from CAS suggests that a quality computing education is no different, that is, making relevant links to other subjects and 'real life'.

The 'how' of computing is learners developing and applying a range of computational thinking skills to gain an understanding or to solve

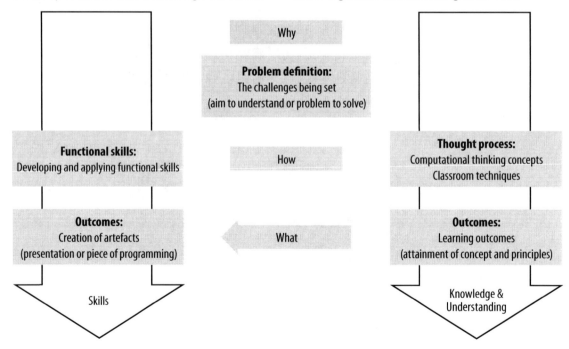

Figure 1: Why, How and What, by Mark Dorling, 2014

problems. This is achieved through the teacher employing a range of computational thinking techniques (approaches) outlined in the CAS computational thinking teachers' guidance and CAS Barefoot Computing.

The 'what' is expressed in the evidence of the actual subject learning. The 'what' matches the learning outcome statements from the CAS Computing Progression Pathways (http://community.computingatschool.org.uk/resources/1692).

Relationship between skills and knowledge
Learners need to develop their skills at the same time as their knowledge and understanding of the subject. It is important to support their future employment and educational needs. They should be developing and using the functional skills of 'how' to use the technology. The solution or product that a learner produces could be a video, podcast, presentation, design, an algorithm, or code to solve a problem is the 'what'. The content for these activities is to be based on the subject content knowledge and the understanding to be developed by the learners. The CAS Computing Progression Pathways describes the detail of the curriculum content which in turn has been developed by considering the associated computational thinking skills. This provides the rationale or 'why' underpinning the lesson.

The challenge, of course, is how to understand the breaths and depth of the curriculum and then plan and assess the resulting lessons.

Understanding breath, depth and progression
The purpose of the Computing Progression Pathways is to support teachers with planning and assessing their learners' attainment and progression in computing. It contains 152 (high level) learning statements covering a commonly agreed interpretation of the breadth and depth of the subject of computing. The column headings

are aligned to the topics found in the CAS's *Computer Science: Curriculum for schools* and Department of Education's *Subject knowledge requirements for entry into computer science teacher training* documents. An alternative version of this framework is available that presents the learning statements by three headings (the 'unofficial' strands of the curriculum outlined in the Royal Society Report *Shut down or Restart*) of Computer Science, Information Technology and Digital Literacy.

The two versions of this framework are shown in tables over the following pages, by topic (pages 168 to 170) and by strand (pages 171 to 173). The original tables are colour coded, but are numbered for the purposes of this book.

The numbering/colour coding correlations are: 1 (Pink), 2 (Yellow), 3 (Orange), 4 (Blue), 5 (Purple), 6 (Red), 7 (Black), and 8 (White).

You will also find these abbreviations useful:
- AL for Algorithm
- DE for Decomposition
- GE for Generalisation (Patterns)
- AB for Abstraction
- EV for Evaluation

Computing Progression Pathways		
Pupil Progression	**Algorithms**	**Programming & Development**
1	• Understands what an algorithm is and is able to express simple linear (non-branching) algorithms symbolically. (AL) • Understands that computers need precise instructions. (AL) • Demonstrates care and precision to avoid errors. (AL)	• Knows that users can develop their own programs, and can demonstrate this by creating a simple program in an environment that does not rely on text *eg* programmable robots *etc* (AL) • Executes, checks and changes programs. (AL) • Understands that programs execute by following precise instructions. (AL)
2	• Understands that algorithms are implemented on digital devices as programs.(AL) • Designs simple algorithms using loops, and selection *ie* if statements. (AL) • Uses logical reasoning to predict outcomes. (AL) • Detects and corrects errors *ie* debugging, in algorithms. (AL)	• Uses arithmetic operators, if statements, and loops, within programs. (AL) • Uses logical reasoning to predict the behaviour of programs. (AL) • Detects and corrects simple semantic errors *ie* debugging, in programs. (AL)
3	• Designs solutions (algorithms) that use repetition and two-way selection *ie* if, then and else. (AL) • Uses diagrams to express solutions. (AB) • Uses logical reasoning to predict outputs, showing an awareness of inputs. (AL)	• Creates programs that implement algorithms to achieve given goals. (AL) • Declares and assigns variables. (AB) • Uses post-tested loop *eg* 'until', and a sequence of selection statements in programs, including an if, then and else statement. (AL)
4	• Shows an awareness of tasks best completed by humans or computers. (EV) • Designs solutions by decomposing a problem and creates a sub-solution for each of these parts. (DE) (AL) (AB) • Recognises that different solutions exist for the same problem. (AL) (AB)	• Understands the difference between, and appropriately uses if and if, then and else statements. (AL) • Uses a variable and relational operators within a loop to govern termination. (AL) (GE) • Designs, writes and debugs modular programs using procedures. (AL) (DE) (AB) (GE) • Knows that a procedure can be used to hide the detail with sub-solution. (AL) (DE) (AB) (GE)
5	• Understands that iteration is the repetition of a process such as a loop. (AL) • Recognises that different algorithms exist for the same problem. (AL) (GE) • Represents solutions using a structured notation. (AL) (AB) • Can identify similarities and differences in situations and can use these to solve problems (pattern recognition). (GE)	• Understands that programming bridges the gap between algorithmic solutions and computers. (AB) • Has practical experience of a high-level textual language, including using standard libraries when programming. (AB) (AL) • Uses a range of operators and expressions *eg* Boolean, and applies them in the context of program control. (AL) • Selects the appropriate data types. (AL) (AB)
6	• Understands a recursive solution to a problem repeatedly applies the same solution to smaller instances of the problem. (AL) (GE) • Recognises that some problems share the same characteristics and use the same algorithm to solve both. (AL) (GE) • Understands the notion of performance for algorithms and appreciates that some algorithms have different performance characteristics for the same task. (AL) (EV)	• Uses nested selection statements. (AL) • Appreciates the need for, and writes, custom functions including use of parameters. (AL) (AB) • Knows the difference between, and uses appropriately, procedures and functions. (AL) (AB) • Understands and uses negation with operators. (AL) • Uses and manipulates one dimensional data structures. (AB) • Detects and corrects syntactical errors. (AL)
7	• Recognises that the design of an algorithm is distinct from its expression in a programming language (which will depend on the programming constructs available). (AL) (AB) • Evaluates the effectiveness of algorithms and models for similar problems. (AL) (AB) (GE) • Recognises where information can be filtered out in generalizing problem solutions. (AL) (AB) (GE) • Uses logical reasoning to explain how an algorithm works. (AL) (AB) (DE) • Represents algorithms using structured language. (AL) (DE) (AB)	• Appreciates the effect of the scope of a variable *eg* a local variable can't be accessed from outside its function. (AB) (AL) • Understands and applies parameter passing. (AB) (GE) (DE) • Understands the difference between, and uses, both pre-tested *eg* 'while', and post-tested *eg* 'until' loops. (AL) • Applies a modular approach to error detection and correction. (AB) (DE) (GE)
8	• Designs a solution to a problem that depends on solutions to smaller instances of the same problem (recursion). (AL) (DE) (AB) (GE) • Understands that some problems cannot be solved computationally. (AB) (GE)	• Designs and writes nested modular programs that enforce reusability utilising sub-routines wherever possible. (AL) (AB) (GE) (DE) • Understands the difference between 'While' loop and 'For' loop, which uses a loop counter. (AL) (AB) • Understands and uses two dimensional data structures. (AB) (DE)

	Computing Progression Pathways	
Pupil Progression	**Data & Data Representation**	**Hardware & Processing**
1	• Recognises that digital content can be represented in many forms. (AB) (GE) • Distinguishes between some of these forms and can explain the different ways that they communicate information. (AB)	• Understands that computers have no intelligence and that computers can do nothing unless a program is executed. (AL) • Recognises that all software executed on digital devices is programmed. (AL) (AB) (GE)
2	• Recognises different types of data: text, number. (AB) (GE) • Appreciates that programs can work with different types of data. (GE) • Recognises that data can be structured in tables to make it useful. (AB) (DE)	• Recognises that a range of digital devices can be considered a computer. (AB) (GE) • Recognises and can use a range of input and output devices. • Understands how programs specify the function of a general purpose computer. (AB)
3	• Understands the difference between data and information. (AB) • Knows why sorting data in a flat file can improve searching for information. (EV) • Uses filters or can perform single criteria searches for information.(AL)	• Knows that computers collect data from various input devices, including sensors and application software. (AB) • Understands the difference between hardware and application software, and their roles within a computer system. (AB)
4	• Performs more complex searches for information eg using Boolean and relational operators. (AL) (GE) (EV) • Analyses and evaluates data and information, and recognises that poor quality data leads to unreliable results, and inaccurate conclusions. (AL) (EV)	• Understands why and when computers are used. (EV) • Understands the main functions of the operating system. (DE) (AB) • Knows the difference between physical, wireless and mobile networks. (AB)
5	• Knows that digital computers use binary to represent all data. (AB) • Understands how bit patterns represent numbers and images. (AB) • Knows that computers transfer data in binary. (AB) • Understands the relationship between binary and file size (uncompressed). (AB) • Defines data types: real numbers and Boolean. (AB) • Queries data on one table using a typical query language. (AB)	• Recognises and understands the function of the main internal parts of basic computer architecture. (AB) • Understands the concepts behind the fetch-execute cycle. (AB) (AL) • Knows that there is a range of operating systems and application software for the same hardware. (AB)
6	• Understands how numbers, images, sounds and character sets use the same bit patterns. (AB) (GE) • Performs simple operations using bit patterns eg binary addition. (AB) (AL) • Understands the relationship between resolution and colour depth, including the effect on file size. (AB) • Distinguishes between data used in a simple program (a variable) and the storage structure for that data. (AB)	• Understands the von Neumann architecture in relation to the fetch-execute cycle, including how data is stored in memory. (AB) (GE) • Understands the basic function and operation of location addressable memory. (AB)
7	• Knows the relationship between data representation and data quality. (AB) • Understands the relationship between binary and electrical circuits, including Boolean logic. (AB) • Understands how and why values are data typed in many different languages when manipulated within programs. (AB)	• Knows that processors have instruction sets and that these relate to low-level instructions carried out by a computer. (AB) (AL) (GE)
8	• Performs operations using bit patterns eg conversion between binary and hexadecimal, binary subtraction etc (AB) (AL) (GE • Understands and can explain the need for data compression, and performs simple compression methods. (AL) (AB) • Knows what a relational database is, and understands the benefits of storing data in multiple tables. (AB) (GE) (DE)	• Has practical experience of a small (hypothetical) low level programming language. (AB) (AL) (DE) (GE) • Understands and can explain Moore's Law. (GE • Understands and can explain multitasking by computers. (AB) (AL) (DE)

Table 1: Computing Progress Pathways – By Topic
Mark Dorling & Matthew Walker, 2013

Computing Progression Pathways		
Pupil Progression	**Communication & Networks**	**Information Technology**
1	• Obtains content from the world wide web using a web browser. (AL) • Understands the importance of communicating safely and respectfully online, and the need for keeping personal information private. (EV) • Knows what to do when concerned about content or being contacted. (AL)	• Uses software under the control of the teacher to create, store and edit digital content using appropriate file and folder names. (AB) (GE) (DE) • Understands that people interact with computers. • Shares their use of technology in school. • Knows common uses of information technology beyond the classroom. (GE) • Talks about their work and makes changes to improve it. (EV)
2	• Navigates the web and can carry out simple web searches to collect digital content. (AL) (EV • Demonstrates use of computers safely and responsibly, knowing a range of ways to report unacceptable content and contact when online.	• Uses technology with increasing independence to purposefully organise digital content. (AB) • Shows an awareness for the quality of digital content collected. (EV) • Uses a variety of software to manipulate and present digital content: data and information. (AL) • Shares their experiences of technology in school and beyond the classroom. (GE) (EV) • Talks about their work and makes improvements to solutions based on feedback received.(EV)
3	• Understands the difference between the internet and internet service eg world wide web. (AB) • Shows an awareness of, and can use a range of internet services eg VOIP. • Recognises what is acceptable and unacceptable behaviour when using technologies and online services.	• Collects, organises and presents data and information in digital content. (AB • Creates digital content to achieve a given goal through combining software packages and internet services to communicate with a wider audience eg blogging. (AL) • Makes appropriate improvements to solutions based on feedback received, and can comment on the success of the solution. (EV)
4	• Understands how to effectively use search engines, and knows how search results are selected, including that search engines use 'web crawler programs'. (AB) (GE) (EV) • Selects, combines and uses internet services. (EV) • Demonstrates responsible use of technologies and online services, and knows a range of ways to report concerns.	• Makes judgements about digital content when evaluating and repurposing it for a given audience. (EV) (GE) • Recognises the audience when designing and creating digital content. (EV) • Understands the potential of information technology for collaboration when computers are networked. (GE) • Uses criteria to evaluate the quality of solutions, can identify improvements making some refinements to the solution, and future solutions. (EV)
5	• Understands how search engines rank search results. (AL) • Understands how to construct static web pages using HTML and CSS. (AL) (AB) • Understands data transmission between digital computers over networks, including the internet ie IP addresses and packet switching. (AL) (AB)	• Evaluates the appropriateness of digital devices, internet services and application software to achieve given goals. (EV) • Recognises ethical issues surrounding the application of information technology beyond school. • Designs criteria to critically evaluate the quality of solutions, uses the criteria to identify improvements and can make appropriate refinements to the solution. (EV)
6	• Knows the names of hardware eg hubs, routers, switches, and the names of protocols eg SMTP, iMAP, POP, FTP, TCP/IP, associated with networking computer systems. (AB) • Uses technologies and online services securely, and knows how to identify and report inappropriate conduct. (AL)	• Justifies the choice of and independently combines and uses multiple digital devices, internet services and application software to achieve given goals. (EV) • Evaluates the trustworthiness of digital content and considers the usability of visual design features when designing and creating digital artifacts for a known audience. (EV) • Identifies and explains how the use of technology can impact on society. • Designs criteria for users to evaluate the quality of solutions, uses the feedback from the users to identify improvements and can make appropriate refinements to the solution. (EV)
7	• Knows the purpose of the hardware and protocols associated with networking computer systems. (AB) (AL) • Understands the client-server model including how dynamic web pages use server-side scripting and that web servers process and store data entered by users. (AL) (AB) (DE) • Recognises that persistence of data on the internet requires careful protection of online identity and privacy.	• Undertakes creative projects that collect, analyse, and evaluate data to meet the needs of a known user group. (AL) (DE) (EV) • Effectively designs and creates digital artefacts for a wider or remote audience. (AL) (DE) • Considers the properties of media when importing them into digital artefacts. (AB) • Documents user feedback, the improvements identified and the refinements made to the solution. (AB) • Explains and justifies how the use of technology impacts on society, from the perspective of social, economical, political, legal, ethical and moral issues. (EV)
8	• Understands the hardware associated with networking computer systems, including WANs and LANs, understands their purpose and how they work, including MAC addresses. (AB) (AL) (DE) (GE)	• Understands the ethical issues surrounding the application of information technology, and the existence of legal frameworks governing its use eg Data Protection Act, Computer Misuse Act, Copyright etc (EV)

Table 1 continued: Computing Progress Pathways – By Topic
Mark Dorling & Matthew Walker, 2013

Computing Progression Pathways	
Mapped to Computer Science, Information Technology and Digital Literacy strands of the National Curriculum Programme of Study	
Pupil Progression	**Computer Science**
1	Understands what an algorithm is and is able to express simple linear (non-branching) algorithms symbolically. Understands that computers need precise instructions. Demonstrates care and precision to avoid errors. Knows that users can develop their own programs, and can demonstrate this by creating a simple program in an environment that does not rely on text *eg* programmable robots *etc*. Executes, checks and changes programs. Understands that programs execute by following precise instructions. Understands that computers have no intelligence and that computers can do nothing unless a program is executed. Recognises that all software executed on digital devices is programmed.
2	Understands that algorithms are implemented on digital devices as programs. Designs simple algorithms using loops, and selection *ie* if statements. Uses logical reasoning to predict outcomes. Detects and corrects errors *ie* debugging, in algorithms. Uses arithmetic operators, if statements, and loops, within programs. Uses logical reasoning to predict the behaviour of programs. Detects and corrects simple semantic errors *ie* debugging, in programs. Recognises that a range of digital devices can be considered a computer. Recognises and can use a range of input and output devices. Understands how programs specify the function of a general purpose computer.
3	Designs solutions (algorithms) that use repetition and two-way selection *ie* if, then and else. Uses diagrams to express solutions. Uses logical reasoning to predict outputs, showing an awareness of inputs. Creates programs that implement algorithms to achieve given goals. Declares and assigns variables. Uses post-tested loop *eg* 'until', and a sequence of selection statements in programs, including an if, then and else statement. Knows that computers collect data from various input devices, including sensors and application software. Understands the difference between hardware and application software, and their roles within a computer system. Understands the difference between the internet and internet service *eg* world wide web.
4	Shows an awareness of tasks best completed by humans or computers. Designs solutions by decomposing a problem and creates a sub-solution for each of these parts (decomposition). Recognises that different solutions exist for the same problem. Understands the difference between, and appropriately uses if and if, then and else statements. Uses a variable and relational operators within a loop to govern termination. Designs, writes and debugs modular programs using procedures. Knows that a procedure can be used to hide the detail with sub-solution (procedural abstraction). Understands why and when computers are used. Understands the main functions of the operating system. Understands how to effectively use search engines, and knows how search results are selected, including that search engines use 'web crawler programs'.
5	Understands that iteration is the repetition of a process such as a loop. Recognises that different algorithms exist for the same problem. Represents solutions using a structured notation. Can identify similarities and differences in situations and can use these to solve problems (pattern recognition). Understands that programming bridges the gap between algorithmic solutions and computers. Has practical experience of a high-level textual language, including using standard libraries when programming. Uses a range of operators and expressions *eg* Boolean, and applies them in the context of program control. Selects the appropriate data types. Defines data types: real numbers and Boolean. Know that digital computers use binary to represent all data. Understand how bit patterns represent numbers and images. Know that computers transfer data in binary. Understand the relationship between binary and file size (uncompressed). Recognises and understands the function of the main internal parts of basic computer architecture. Understands the concepts behind the fetch-execute cycle. Understands how search engines rank search results. Understands how to construct static web pages using HTML and CSS. Understands data transmission between digital computers over networks, including the internet *ie* IP addresses and packet switching.
6	Understands a recursive solution to a problem repeatedly applies the same solution to smaller instances of the problem. Recognises that some problems share the same characteristics and use the same algorithm to solve both (generalisation). Understands the notion of performance for algorithms and appreciates that some algorithms have different performance characteristics for the same task. Uses nested selection statements. Appreciates the need for, and writes, custom functions including use of parameters. Knows the difference between, and uses appropriately, procedures and functions. Understands and uses negation with operators. Uses and manipulates one dimensional data structures. Detects and corrects syntactical errors. Understands how numbers, images, sounds and character sets use the same bit patterns. Performs simple operations using bit patterns *eg* binary addition. Understands the relationship between resolution and colour depth, including the effect on file size. Distinguishes between data used in a simple program (a variable) and the storage structure for that data. Understands the von Neumann architecture in relation to the fetch-execute cycle, including how data is stored in memory. Understands the basic function and operation of location addressable memory.
7	Recognises that the design of an algorithm is distinct from its expression in a programming language (which will depend on the programming constructs available). Evaluates the effectiveness of algorithms and models for similar problems. Recognises where information can be filtered out in generalizing problem solutions (abraction). Uses logical reasoning to explain how an algorithm works. Represents algorithms using structured language. Appreciates the effect of the scope of a variable *eg* a local variable can't be accessed from outside its function. Understands and applies parameter passing. Understands the difference between, and uses, both pre-tested *eg* 'while', and post-tested *eg* 'until' loops. Applies a modular approach to error detection and correction. Knows the relationship between data representation and data quality. Understands the relationship between binary and electrical circuits, including Boolean logic. Understands how and why values are data typed in many different languages when manipulated within programs. Knows that processors have instruction sets and that these relate to low-level instructions carried out by a computer. Understands the client-server model including how dynamic web pages use server-side scripting and that web servers process and store data entered by users.
8	Designs a solution to a problem that depends on solutions to smaller instances of the same problem (recursion). Understands that some problems cannot be solved computationally. Designs and writes nested modular programs that enforce reusability utilising sub-routines where ever possible. Understands the difference between 'While' loop and 'For' loop, which uses a loop counter. Understands and uses two dimensional data structures. Performs operations using bit patterns *eg* conversion between binary and hexadecimal, binary subtraction *etc*. Understands and can explain the need for data compression, and performs simple compression methods. Has practical experience of a small (hypothetical) low level programming language. Understands and can explain Moore's Law. Understands and can explain multitasking by computers.

Table 2: Computing Progress Pathways – By Strand
Mark Dorling & Matthew Walker, 2013

Computing Progression Pathways	
Mapped to Computer Science, Information Technology and Digital Literacy strands of the National Curriculum Programme of Study	
Pupil Progression	**Information Technology**
1	Recognises that digital content can be represented in many forms. Distinguishes between some of these forms and can explain the different ways that they communicate information. Obtains content from the world wide web using a web browser. Uses software under the control of the teacher to create, store and edit digital content using appropriate file and folder names. Understands that people interact with computers. Talks about their work and makes changes to improve it.
2	Recognises different types of data: text, number. Appreciates that programs can work with different types of data. Recognises that data can be structured in tables to make it useful. Recognises that a range of digital devices can be considered a computer. Recognises and can use a range of input and output devices. Navigates the web and can carry out simple web searches to collect digital content. Uses technology with increasing independence to purposefully organise digital content. Uses a variety of software to manipulate and present digital content: data and information. Shares their experiences of technology in school and beyond the classroom. Talks about their work and makes improvements to solutions based on feedback received.
3	Understands the difference between data and information. Knows why sorting data in a flat file can improve searching for information. Using filters or can perform single criteria searches for information. Shows an awareness of, and can use a range of internet services *eg* VOIP. Collects, organises and presents data and information in digital content. Creates digital content to achieve a given goal through combining software packages and internet services to communicate with a wider audience *eg* blogging. Makes appropriate improvements to solutions based on feedback received, and can comment on the success of the solution.
4	Performs more complex searches for information *eg* using Boolean and relational operators. Analyses and evaluates data and information, and recognises that poor quality data leads to unreliable results, and inaccurate conclusions. Knows the difference between physical, wireless and mobile networks. Recognises the audience when designing and creating digital content. Uses criteria to evaluate the quality of solutions, can identify improvements making some refinements to the solution, and future solutions.
5	Queries data on one table using a typical query language. Knows that there is a range of operating systems and application software for the same hardware. Evaluates the appropriateness of digital devices, internet services and application software to achieve given goals. Designs criteria to critically evaluate the quality of solutions, uses the criteria to identify improvements and can make appropriate refinements to the solution.
6	Knows the names of hardware *eg* hubs, routers, switches, and the names of protocols *eg* SMTP, iMAP, POP, FTP, TCP/IP, associated with networking computer systems. Justifies the choice of and independently combines and uses multiple digital devices, internet services and application software to achieve given goals. Evaluates the trustworthiness of digital content and considers the usability of visual design features when designing and creating digital artifacts for a known audience. Designs criteria for users to evaluate the quality of solutions, uses the feedback from the users to identify improvements and can make appropriate refinements to the solution.
7	Knows the purpose of the hardware and protocols associated with networking computer systems. Undertakes creative projects that collect, analyse, and evaluate data to meet the needs of a known user group. Effectively designs and creates digital artefacts for a wider or remote audience. Considers the properties of media when importing them into digital artefacts. Documents user feedback, the improvements identified and the refinement made to the solution.
8	Knows what a relational database is, and understands the benefits of storing data in multiple tables. Understands the hardware associated with networking computer systems, including WANs and LANs, understands their purpose and how they work, including MAC addresses.

Table 2 continued: Computing Progress Pathways – By Strand
Mark Dorling & Matthew Walker, 2013

Pupil Progression	Computing Progression Pathways Mapped to Computer Science, Information Technology and Digital Literacy strands of the National Curriculum Programme of Study
	Digital literacy
1	Understands the importance of communicating safely and respectfully online, and the need for keeping personal information private. Knows what to do when concerned about content or being contacted. Knows common uses of information technology beyond the classroom. Shares their use of technology in school.
2	Demonstrates use of computers safely and responsibly, knowing a range of ways to report unacceptable content and contact when online. Shows an awareness for the quality of digital content collected.
3	Recognises what is acceptable and unacceptable behaviour when using technologies and online services.
4	Makes judgements about digital content when evaluating and repurposing it for a given audience. Demonstrates responsible use of technologies and online services, and knows a range of ways to report concerns. Selects, combines and uses internet services. Understands the potential of information technology for collaboration when computers are networked.
5	Recognises ethical issues surrounding the application of information technology beyond school.
6	Uses technologies and online services securely, and knows how to identify and report inappropriate conduct. Identifies and explains how the use of technology can impact on society.
7	Recognises that persistence of data on the internet requires careful protection of online identity and privacy. Explains and justifies how the use of technology impacts on society, from the perspective of social, economical, political, legal, ethical and moral issues.
8	Understands the ethical issues surrounding the application of information technology, and the existence of legal frameworks governing its use *eg* Data Protection Act, Computer Misuse Act, Copyright *etc*.

The learning statements and defined progression have also been aligned to the CAS Primary and CAS Secondary guidance documents.

The progression through each topic (column) of computing is broken down into rows. The rows are colour coded (numbered on these pages) to help the teacher to assess whether learners are showing progression of competency *ie* knowledge and skills, and recognise achievement or attainment. It is suggested that:

- Primary teachers focus on the learning statements from the pink (1) to purple (5) row.
- Secondary teachers focus on the learning statements from the purple (5) to black row (7).
- The white row (8) overlaps with the Key Stage 4 qualification specifications.

The learning statement within a given topic colour (column/row) are not weighted. The emphasis is on skills, knowledge and understanding, and the dependencies and interdependencies between learning statements. The topic colours (rows) *eg* Algorithms Blue, are not allocated to particular key stages or year groups; the emphasis is on 'continued learning' and meaningful progression through and across all the strands of computing. The relationship is between individual learning statements and the National Curriculum Programme of Study statements.

The use of Bloom's Taxonomy in the wording of the learning statements is designed to provide a steer to teachers on the granular learning outcomes (and associated activities) required to complete a given learning statement within a particular topic colour.

It is not intended that schools use the order that the learning statements are presented within a topic colour or the assigned Bloom's Taxonomy value to attribute a weighting to the learning statements to use them as attainment values or sub-levels nor use the order in which the learning statements are presented to teach the principles and concepts because there are dependencies and interdependencies both vertically and horizontally between learning statement.

Those schools planning to use the CAS Computing Progression Pathways with their existing assessment/reporting system should agree a benchmark 'level' for the learners entering a particular year group or key stage, assigning a arbitrary benchmark value (level, colour, symbol, shape, character or number) to the appropriate progression statements for each strand.

For schools using a system to set targets for computing based on performance in other subjects then the flexibility of the CAS Computing Progression Pathways framework is that it allows schools to adjust the values (levels) you choose to assign to the coloured rows.

Schools may decide that learners entering a particular key stage have prior learning to suggest that they are on the yellow and orange rows for the various strands shown in the grid. If this is the case then you would start your teaching at the appropriate level of learning statement and assign the arbitrary assessment/reporting values accordingly.

Use with Digital Badges (optional)
Each topic heading (column) can be assigned a different Digital Badge, for example, a Rubik's cube might represent the 'Algorithms' topic. As learners progress through the topic colours, the Digital Badge design remains the same but the colour of the Digital Badge would change to reflect achievement and progression. For

example, sets of Digital Badges created by the community visit the CAS Community website.

Using this system of Digital Badges, if learners are working between two colours (rows) for a particular badge *eg* orange and blue, then it is suggested that a two-tone badge is available so that you can record and reward sub levels of progress and attainment.

Alternatively, you might choose to combine learning statements from different topic colours into a custom Digital Badge that relates to a curricular or extra-curricular project or challenge with a greater emphasis placed on the 'why' of the learning *ie* the challenge, rather than the 'what' *ie* the knowledge and skills from the CAS Computing Progression Pathways. For examples of these types of Digital Badge projects, you can visit the *Makewav.es* website.

There are currently no Digital Badge designs for the topic (column) headers. The authors of the CAS Computing Progression Pathways believe that the teachers and learners who would be using the Digital Badge system would be much better placed to design and create them. It is hoped that the process of designing and creating the Digital Badges will engender a greater ownership of the rewards system by your learners, in your school.

PLANNING SCHEMES OF WORK AND LESSONS

Writing lesson plans that focus on computational thinking

The planning, teaching and evaluation cycle is recognised as good practice. The planning phase of this cycle needs to be slightly adjusted, to ensure that lessons are underpinned by computational thinking. This means a four-step cycle to planning lessons with computational thinking embedded, the first three of the four steps of which are already explicit in teachers planning process; it is the fourth step that is new to teachers.

The four steps of the lesson planning process are:

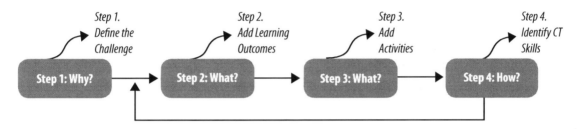

Note: Repeat this process for each of
the lessons in your learning journey

Figure 2: Paul Curzon, Mark Dorling, Thomas Ng, Cynthia Selby, and John Woollard 2014

The evaluation of lessons and the assessment of pupil progress will feed back to Step 2 to 4, determining the next 'what' of the curriculum.

Planning a Learning Journey (Scheme of Work)

Begin by watching Miles Berry in the DfE funded CAS QuickStart Computing on taking your first steps towards developing your Computing Curriculum.

As suggested, begin by reviewing your existing schemes of work for curriculum coverage. Then decide which of your Learning Journeys need to be:

*   removed because they do not meet any of the learning outcomes associated with the Computing Curriculum;

http://primary.quickstartcomputing.org/resources/mp4/planning_sow.mp4

- adapted so that they meet the learning outcomes; or
- supplemented, especially with the learning outcomes associated with computational thinking.

Planning Process – Step 1: Defining the Challenge

To encourage engagement, identify a real world focus for activities, ideally by making relevant cross curriculum links to other subjects. These should be gender-neutral where appropriate. The real world context might be about technology, people or both.

This should give motivation to all learners in the sense of 'Why is this area important to understand?' or 'Why is this problem a useful one to solve?'. The 'why' for learners should be deeper than 'because the teacher says I have to learn it'.

The learners are a great source of inspiration for identifying real life focuses for schemes of work as it is important that they relate to the real world context. Why not also read Computer Science for Fun (CS4FN) or work with local secondary specialist teachers, academics and industry

Example: teaching computing through dance

www.quickstartcomputing.org/secondary/
Teaching-computing-through-dance.html

professionals, who are excellent sources of ideas and can support for your planning.

It is important to choose appropriate and scalable challenges that incorporate relevant hooks for the learners.

Example: Rising Stars Switched On series aimed at primary school aged pupils

> **INTRODUCTION**
>
> In this unit, the children will relate algorithms to recipes. They will write a recipe for a healthy sandwich and use this to create an electronic recipe book, which will also include photos and audio instructions.

In this example, the 'why' can be described in a way that shows relevance to learners' everyday lives. For primary school age learners this may relate to daily tasks, such as following a recipe, devising a storyboard or giving a set of instructions to carry out a task like 'which way do you go home?'.

Another example of this approach has been captured in a Department for Education video focused on The Teaching of Computing Through Dance. It exemplifies one of the goals of education: to encourage and empower learners to take responsibility for their own learning and develop confidence in both computing and computational thinking.

This can be achieved through project based learning both individually and collaboratively. Learners ask questions and understand why particular topics are being taught, regardless of the subject.

Planning Process – Step 2: Adding Learning Outcomes

Determine the 'what' – Learning Outcomes

The Learning Outcomes for your lessons are drawn from the National Curriculum or at a more granular level using the CAS Computing Progression Pathways (http://community. computingatschool.org.uk/resources/1692).

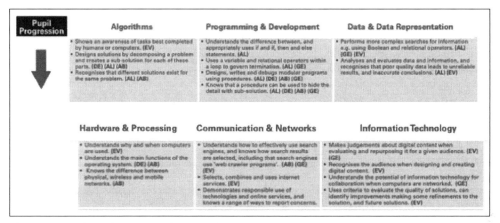

Figure 2: Mark Dorling & Matthew Walker 2013

Relevant learning statements are identified by considering the learners' prior experience and attainment. It should enable learners to move closer to completing or achieving the 'why' from The Planning Process – Step 1: Defining the challenge.

There might be multiple learning outcomes for each of the 152 high level learning statements from the CAS Computing Progression Pathways. For further support on identifying relevant learning outcomes, you could access a list of 1100+ learning outcomes by registering for free at www.progression-pathways.co.uk. An example, of this is at:

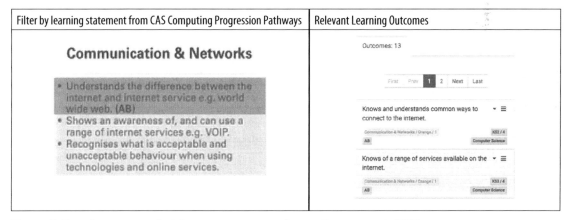

Figure 3: Based on screen shot from www.progression-pathways.co.uk, 2015

Planning Process – Step 3: Adding Activities

Determine the 'what' – Activities
Once you have identified the learning outcomes it is important to identify appropriate activities to support this learning.

You might have multiple activities to be undertaken by learners to achieve either learning outcomes identified or the high level learning statements from the CAS Computing Progression Pathways. For further support on identifying relevant activities, you could access a list of 1400+ activities by registering for free at www.progression-pathways.co.uk. An example, of this is at:

Filter by learning statement from CAS Computing Progression Pathways	Relevant Learning Activities
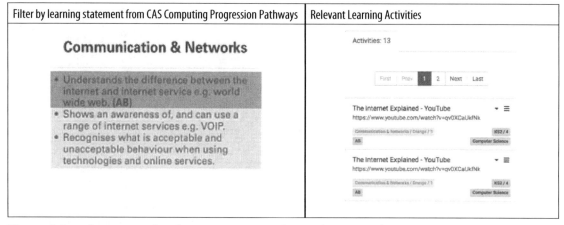	

Figure 4: Based on screen shot from www.progression-pathways.co.uk, 2015

Alternatively, you could seek inspiration from various commercial and non-commercial education suppliers, for example:

*   CAS Barefoot Computing project (www.barefootcas.org.uk)
*   Code Club (www.codeclub.org.uk)
*   Code-It (www.code-it.co.uk)
*   Digital Schoolhouse (www. digitalschoolhouse.org.uk)

Planning Process – Step 4: Identifying Computational Thinking Skills

Identifying Computational Thinking Skills
This is the extra step in the planning process that needs to be completed to meet the aims of the National Curriculum to embed computational thinking.

The relationship is between the computational thinking skills and the activity chosen by the teacher to meet the learning outcome.

The computational thinking skill concepts are already identified and mapped in the CAS Computing Progression Pathways. The CAS computational thinking teacher guidance document (http://community.computingatschool. org.uk/resources/2324) explains the concepts and the specific computational thinking techniques and approaches. The Computing Progression Pathways incorporates the concepts of computational thinking using the initials:

*   AL for Algorithm
*   DE for Decomposition

- GE for Generalisation (Patterns)
- AB for Abstraction
- EV for Evaluation

After selecting an activity you now need to evaluate that activity for the computational thinking opportunities. Use the mapping from Step 3 of the planning process combined with the CAS Computing Progression Pathways to direct you to the appropriate list of techniques/approaches listed in the CAS computational thinking teacher guidance, essentially to determine the 'how'. The image below illustrates the list of techniques/approaches that were identified by a teacher from an example activity.

Which 'Evaluation' classroom techniques?

Evaluation

- Making judgements based on external criteria
- Making trade-offs between competing requirements
- Making judgements about effectiveness (When is good enough good enough?)
- Making comparisons and reaching conclusions
- Interpretation of test results

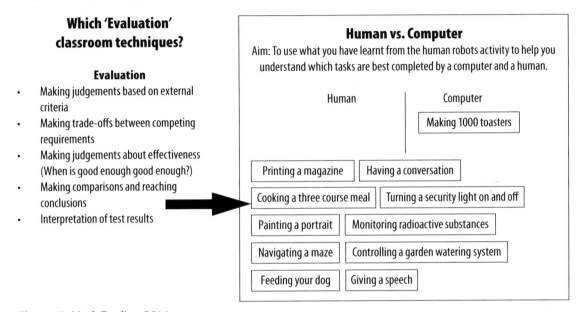

Figure 5: Mark Dorling 2014

The importance of this step and the benefits when assessing the learners' attainment and progress is explained later in the chapter.

For further support on automating this step of the planning process *ie* identifying the computational thinking techniques/approaches for the activities, you could register for free at www.progression-pathways.co.uk. For example, the activity in the lesson below maps to Algorithms/Pink/Statement 2 (Understands that computers need precise instructions). That statement is aligned to Algorithmic Thinking. Clicking the toggle for Algorithmic Thinking (displayed on figure overleaf) presents you with all the associated computational thinking techniques/approaches to choose from.

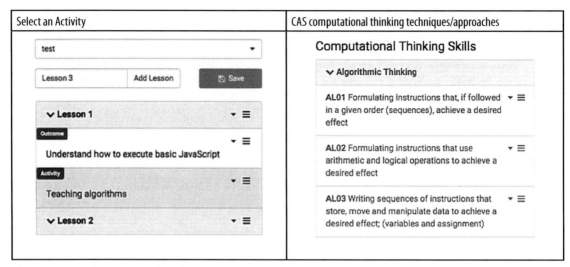

Select an Activity	CAS computational thinking techniques/approaches

Figure 6: Based on screen shot from www.progression-pathways.co.uk, 2015

It is important to note that every teacher could potentially identify different computational thinking techniques/approaches depending upon how they planned to deliver it to activity with their class and what thinking skills they, the learners, need to develop. When delivering the lesson, you might also find that through your key questioning that your learners will naturally need and want to develop computational thinking skills that you had overlooked, therefore, it is important to return to update your planning to reflect this, the significance of which will become apparent in the chapter on assessment.

RECORDING AND ASSESSING COMPUTING AND COMPUTATIONAL THINKING

Recording progression and attainment

The artefacts (completed activities) that learners produce should be evaluated against both the 'why' and the 'what':

1. Consider the artefact against the intended Learning Outcome. If it demonstrates different Learning Outcomes than you intended, does the learner justify what they did? This will enable you to make a judgement based on they learner's learning profile.

2. If you are marking an extended piece of work *eg* a project, is the artefact produced fit for purpose against the hook of the project i.e. the 'why'.

It is recognized good practice in primary education to record progression and attainment through a simple traffic light system. For example:

Colour traffic light	Suggested meaning
	Not assessed – learner has yet to be assessed or was absent.
	Target – learner has been introduced to an outcome/activity but more work needs to be done.
	Working towards – learner is working towards or part met an outcome/activity.
	Met – learner has secured and consolidated an outcome/activity.

Colour key:

Grey   Red   Amber   Green

It is recognised as good practice to regularly assess and record the learners' attainment from completing activities via the artefacts they produce. Because both Learning Outcomes (Planning process – Step 2) and Activities (Planning process – Step 3) are mapped to the CAS Computing Progression Pathways statements, which in turn are mapped to the computational thinking skills from the CAS Computational Thinking Teachers' Guidance enables you to build profiles of both the learners' attainment of the competencies *ie* knowledge and skills, and their computational thinking capabilities.

	Graham	Jim	Monty	Mark
Lesson 1: Commands, causes and effect and parameters				
Outcome Understand how to execute basic JavaScript	⚪	⚪	⚪	⚪
Activity Using commands	⚫	⚫	⚫	⚫
Introduce cause and effect	⚫	⚫	⚫	⚫

Colour key:

Grey   Red   Amber   Green

Figure 7: Based on screen shot from www.progression-pathways.co.uk, 2015

Assessing computing and computational thinking

Whether you choose to assess a learner's attainment and progression by the National Curriculum programme of study or at a more granular level using the CAS Computing Progression Pathways, the important thing is to record progression of both computing and computational thinking over a sustained period of time.

National Curriculum

	Visited	Avg. Score	Last 3 Visited	Last 3 Avg. Score
KS1/1 Understanding what algorithms are; how they are implemented as programs on digital devices; and that programs execute by following precise and unambiguous instructions.	2	2.50	2	2.50

CAS Progression Pathways

	Visited	Avg. Score	Last 3 Visited	Last 3 Avg. Score
Algorithms/Pink/2 Understanding that computers need precise instructions.	2	2.50	2	2.50

Figure 8: Based on screen shot from www.progression-pathways.co.uk 2015

The image below shows the average attainment score and colour (out of 3) for all the times that a learner has covered that given learning statement. Attainment and progression can be identified by comparing the Average Overall Score against the Average Score for the last three times a learner has covered a given statement. For example, a change from amber (1.83) to green (2.50) shows a learner is making good progress.

A deteriorating score may suggest to the teacher that an intervention (further support) may be needed.

When deterioration in progress occurs, the teacher could examine a learner's computational thinking profile to identify specific computational thinking skills that might be preventing the learner from progressing.

Visited	Avg. Score	Last 3 Visited	Last 3 Avg. Score
6	1.83	3	2.50

Figure 9: Screen shot from www.progression-pathways.co.uk 2015

Therefore, it is important to build a holistic understanding of how learners apply computational thinking skills to a range of classroom activities. Over a period of time, it is possible for teachers to identify patterns in the activities in which learners struggle to complete successfully (or vice versa). By mapping and recording the associations between the activity and the computational thinking opportunities, it is possible to identify 'indicators' for the computational thinking skills where learners appear to be weaker (or stronger).

One way of achieving this is through recording the computational thinking opportunities during the planning process described previously, for a range of classroom activities within your Scheme of Work.

There are two levels of association between activities and computational thinking you can choose from, depending upon the detail you require:

High level
Associations between Activities and Computational Thinking concepts of Abstraction, Algorithmic Thinking, Decomposition, Evaluation, and Generalisation (pattern matching). This is done for you through the mapping of activities to statements in the CAS Computing Progression Pathways. (see figure overleaf).

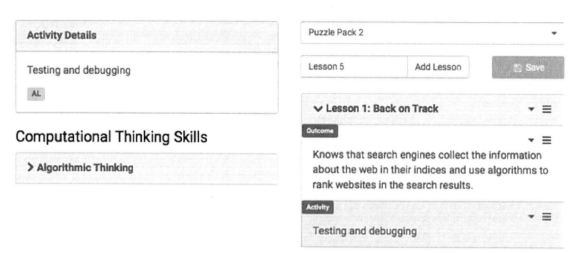

Figure 10: Based on screen shot from www.progression-pathways.co.uk, 2015

This level of association will produce a learner profile showing the attainment and progression for computational thinking at a 'concept' level. For example, looking at the screen shot below, it would suggest that the learner is making progress in Algorithmic Thinking skills but still 'working towards' Abstraction skills.

Although this high level of association between

Activities and computational thinking will save you time in the planning process and will provide you with some understanding of the learners computational thinking capabilities; this level of association will not empower you to know exactly which of the Abstraction techniques/approaches the learner is struggling with, making possible interventions (support) less targeted and potentially less effective.

CAS Computational Thinking

Abstraction	Visited	Avg. Score	Last 3 Visited	Last 3 Avg. Score
	6	2.00	3	1.83
Algorithmic Thinking	Visited	Avg. Score	Last 3 Visited	Last 3 Avg. Score
	6	1.83	3	2.50

Figure 11: Based on screen shot from www.progression-pathways.co.uk, 2015

Granular level

Associations between Activities and the computational thinking skills techniques/

approaches (Planning process – Step 4) can provide a greater understanding of the learners' capabilities.

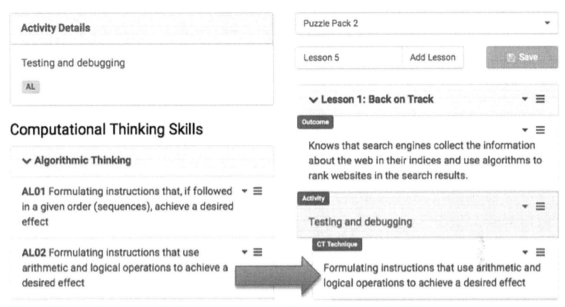

Figure 12: Based on screenshot from www.progression-pathways.co.uk, 2015

This level of association will produce a learner profile showing the attainment and progression for computational thinking, at a computational thinking technique/approach level. For example, it would suggest or indicate that the learner is making progress in applying Algorithmic Thinking skills, in particular 'AL02: Formulating instructions that use arithmetic and logical operations to achieve a desired effect' but is still 'working towards' Abstraction skills, in particular, 'AB01: Reducing complexity by removing unnecessary detail'.

How will the data in assess IT for computational thinking help my learners?

Given sufficient time in the classroom with learners, formative assessment can be an incredibly useful tool. It involves observing and

discussing with learners how they developed a particular understanding of a problem or solution. For example, discussing how learners explain and justify the process (use of computational thinking) they went through.

This will however only provide a snap shot of how learners applied computational thinking to that specific problem. This is no guarantee that they will demonstrate the same competency to future activities that require similar computational thinking skills to be applied.

This holistic understanding of the learners computational thinking abilities from the planning, recording and assessing process described in this chapter could make the use of formative assessment more useful, as a prediction of the types of activities where the learner is likely to struggle *eg* abstraction, and make any interventions (support in computational thinking skills) more targeted and timely. This in time should reflect in an improvement in the learner's capability and attainment (grades).

Using this data in your school reporting systems

School reporting systems will take time to change and adapt to new and innovative ways of assessing and reporting learners attainment and progression. The CAS Computing Progression Pathways and computational thinking framework outlined in the CAS computational thinking teachers' guidance will help provide a learning profile of learners' attainment and progression, either by the six computing topics or the three 'unofficial' strands of the curriculum; enabling the teacher to use this assessment information to make a professional judgment about the learners overall attainment and progression across the subject of computing and computational thinking in a format that suits their school reporting systems.